ORAGE WITH GURDJIEFF
IN AMERICA

Louise Welch

ORAGE WITH GURDJIEFF IN AMERICA

ROUTLEDGE & KEGAN PAUL
Boston, London, Melbourne and Henley

First published in 1982
by Routledge & Kegan Paul Ltd
9 Park Street, Boston, Mass. 02108, USA,
39 Store Street, London WC1E 7DD,
296 Beaconsfield Parade,
Middle Park, Melbourne, 3206, Australia and
Broadway House, Newtown Road
Henley-on-Thames, Oxon. RE9 1EN
Set in 10/12 Garamond by
Input Typesetting Ltd, London
and printed in the USA

Library of Congress Cataloging in Publication Data

Welch, Louise.

Orage with Gurdjieff in America.

Includes bibliographical references.
1. Gurdjieff, Georges Ivanovitch,
1872–1949. 2. Orage, A. R. (Alfred
Richard), 1873–1934. I. Title.
B4249.G84W44   133'.092'2   82–3808
ISBN 0–7100–9016–1   AACR2

For Cordelia, Patricia Louise,
Suzanna Louise, Thalía,
Thomas and Fernando.

CONTENTS

Acknowledgments

To give thanks for the help I received in preparing this memoir of Orage, I will begin by reviewing my occasions for gratitude to those who are no longer alive or, as Gurdjieff might say, no longer on the planet Earth. Thanks first to Melville Cane, lawyer and poet, who in his hundredth year took the trouble to write me a letter by hand, and was kind enough to talk with me shortly before his death. Next, thanks are due to the concert pianist, Carol Robinson, who played the Gurdjieff music when I first heard it and set a standard for its performance, who talked with me at length about her experiences both with Orage and with his teacher in America and Fontainebleau. Rosemary Nott (Mrs C. S. Nott), also a gifted pianist, on her last visit to New York reviewed with me her time at the Prieuré and the early days with Orage. Her husband, Stanley, both before and after the publication of his books on Gurdjieff, filled me in with his recollections. Poet Jean Toomer, also one of Orage's helpers, wrote an account, especially for Dr Welch, on his first days at the Prieuré. He left many letters to Fiske University. Allan Brown, whose widow made available his letters from Orage, is to be thanked. Unbounded appreciation is due Israel Solon, whose letters from Orage tell better than anything else Orage's view of his own dilemma. Would that Edna Kenton were here as helper and critic! As her notes were gratefully acknowledged by Leon Edel with regard to his excellent, five-volume biography of Henry James, so are the careful notes she took of the Orage meetings.

To turn to the living, recognition is owed Jessmin Howarth, chosen by Gurdjieff to teach his sacred dances, who continues with them to this day, and is regarded as an authority, often consulted by those who wish to study the authentic material. Poet Mavis McIntosh is to be thanked, among other things, for her full and accurate notes of the Orage meetings, her many recollections, and for the anecdote that appears in this book. Lawrence S. Morris provided invaluable notes, gave the manuscript several readings, making suggestions that were of enormous help. It must be said here that some currency has been given to the statement that no notes of Orage's meetings were taken verbatim. This is just not so. The notes referred to in this book were taken as he spoke, with Orage's permission, as were my own. It was Gurdjieff, according to P. D. Ouspensky, who forbade the taking of notes during his talks.

Others who gave me access to their letters from Orage include John Riordan and Adam Nott, who sent me many of his father's. Among Orage's American friends who responded generously to interviews were Lisa Delza (Mrs Gorham Munson), whose husband was another of Orage's official helpers. Many thanks to my old friend, Jessie Orage, whose reminiscences reminded me of much that I had forgotten. Her son, Richard, too young at his father's death to remember much, nevertheless had valuable early impressions.

Among those who lightened the heavy burden of research was Lisa Paloheimo, who wrote her master's thesis on Orage at the University of Toronto, dug relentlessly into all possible material, and made it available. My daughter, Martha de Llosa, was endlessly helpful as editor and critic, which role she shared with my husband. Thanks also to Martha P. Heyneman, a subtle flaw discoverer, and to P. L. Travers, who encouraged me to continue. Kathy Maroko typed the manuscript often and with patience. It is impossible to say adequately how grateful I am to all these friends, living and dead, and to many others who supported my effort. For errors and oversights that may appear, no one but myself is to blame.

Introduction

In 1922, A. R. Orage, then in his fiftieth year and at the crest of his career as editor of London's most influential literary journal, the *New Age*, abruptly laid aside his pencil, said farewell to his stunned colleagues, and disappeared into the forest of Fontainebleau. His destination was the Prieuré, a seventeenth-century château near the village of Avon, where G. I. Gurdjieff had established his Institute for the Harmonious Development of Man. Orage had heard about it through P. D. Ouspensky, whose groups he had attended for more than a year. At that point Orage had no way of knowing that fourteen months later he would be in the United States preparing the new world for Gurdjieff's visit.

Little sympathy existed then for a crisis of the spirit in the dogmatic intellectual climate of the twenties. Few were hospitable to an unknown spiritual teaching rooted in timeless esoteric ideas; it would require to be presented in a form suited to Western mentality.

Nor were matters helped by the appearance of its founder, G. I. Gurdjieff, a stocky, swarthy, shaven-headed, heavily-mustached Georgian, handsome in his way but definitely not Western. His behavior, too, seemed incomprehensible, since it was soon evident that he was indifferent to what people thought of him. He came to shock us awake, and shock us he did.

Now, half a century later, the man and his teaching are revered by many serious people in search of meaning and method. They are grateful to the unique intelligence that has led them to a new understanding of the tragic elements of life – what Gurdjieff called 'the terror of the situation.'

This was by no means the case in 1924, when Gurdjieff first came to America, where Orage had already become his spokesman. Today, in large part owing to Orage's luminous exposition of Gurdjieff's subtle thought, there are more people in America engaged in the study of his teaching than in any other country.

Since those early beginnings, thousands of people have encountered Gurdjieff's world-view and many interpreters have appeared. But there are also many who are not aware of the part played by Orage, the gifted editor and writer.

His impact was great and he was content to let the evidence show in the deepened understanding of those who studied with him, and in the enrichment of their lives. Since, however, he was primarily responsible for the welcome given the Gurdjieff teaching by discriminating people, those of us with vivid memories of the Oragean days feel that their special quality must not be lost to posterity.

In England, where Orage was loved and admired, much has been written about him as writer, editor, teacher and friend. Very little has been said, however, of his life and influence in America, where Orage said he had found the nearest thing to brotherhood he had ever known. I hope the pages that follow will serve, in some measure, to fill the gap.

1
Arrival in America

It cannot be the will of God that free intelligence should be extinguished from the planet; the world, somehow or other, must be made safe for intelligence as for democracy.   A. R. ORAGE

'I expect to be sailing for New York on December 15 to spend a few weeks in preparing the way for Mr Gurdjieff's visit in January,' Orage wrote to Claude Bragdon in 1923. 'Naturally I should come with even more timidity if I did not expect to find you there . . . I should be most grateful if you would collect such material as might be useful to my mission. Your friends, I feel, are bound to be friends of the Institute.'[1] Whatever else, Orage needed the American friends he had made on the *New Age*, and was hopeful of their response to the Gurdjieff teaching.

When he arrived in New York in late December, he went straight from the boat to the office of the *Little Review* on East Eleventh Street, near Fifth Avenue, where its founders and editors, Margaret Anderson and Jane Heap, awaited him. They had been friends by letter for some years. Orage had sent them a long piece for the Henry James number of their journal of August 1918.[2]

Soon telephones began ringing at studios and literary warrens in Greenwich Village and Chelsea to inform the world of arts and letters that Orage had arrived. Many hurried from their studios and offices to welcome him. Before the week was out, literary critic Gorham Munson was in touch with more of the friends Orage wished to reach, literary, philosophical or artistic, who were apt to be more open than most to unconventional ideas.

'We must start at once,' Orage said, with a toss of the head, as he taxied with some of his newly made friends to the Sunwise

Turn bookshop, near the Yale Club on Forty-fourth Street. Jessie Dwight, patrician sales clerk and part-owner, greeted him warmly. Tall, fair-haired, handsome and hardly half his age, the strong-minded scion of generations of Connecticut clergymen and scholars, she fell in love with him at sight. She not only welcomed him but began calling people on her list. For years they had been coming to the bookshop to buy the *New Age* and would, of course, listen to what he had to say about Gurdjieff.

A few days later Orage faced his first American audience at the crowded Sunwise Turn. Gurdjieff, he told them, a true teacher, was on his way to New York. One of the few survivors of a group of men who called themselves seekers after truth, Gurdjieff had worked, studied, experienced, and now assembled a teaching based on esoteric knowledge, which he had re-searched, tested and verified in himself over many years. At last, he had returned to Europe to bring Eastern wisdom to Western knowledge.

With his first European pupils, Gurdjieff had worked in Mos-cow and St Petersburg, but soon the 1917 revolution had made it impossible to stay there, and they moved to parts of Russia not yet rendered unlivable. By the summer of 1918 they had to flee again, and Gurdjieff led them away from Essentuki over a mountain pass. First they were in Tiflis, then Turkey, Germany and finally, France, where at last he set up his long-planned Institute for the Harmonious Development of Man.

With a lilt of promise in his voice, Orage spoke of Gurdjieff's view of the present state of the human psyche, which modern life with its comforts, conveniences and complexities failed to nourish. Those wishing wholeness, he said, which is essentially 'holiness', must undertake a discipline and a work.

Two kinds of people, he went on, could become interested in work for inner evolution: those concerned mainly with theory, who would become scholars of the work, and those concerned with practice, who with training and help could hope to achieve a new level of being. Both kinds were active at the Prieuré.

The impression Orage made on those who heard him in De-cember 1923, was of an engaging, witty and deeply serious man. Some have described his quiet demeanor and his burning dark eyes as they responded with deep courtesy to every questioner. Daly King's first view of Orage showed him a tall and slender man, dressed inconspicuously in a dark business suit, who struck him with the complete and utter rationality of what he said:[3]

> The topics went to the real heart of what had always intrigued me, those questions which I had always hitherto found hedged about by qualifications, half-statements, sometimes even a shame-faced avoidance, always a lack of specificity which had convinced me that the speaker didn't actually know the truth about such subjects. I was not merely fascinated; I received such an interior lift of pure exaltation at the discovery that these questions could be considered seriously, fully and without equivocation . . . To cap it all was the assurance of scepticism, the rational demand that I must *not* believe until I myself had obtained the proof.

In addition to gathering people to hear Gurdjieff, Orage had also to find temporary rooms for Gurdjieff and his party, by then on the high seas. He settled on the Ansonia, a massive, baroque and somewhat seedy Edwardian hotel at Seventy-third Street and Broadway, not the least of its appointments being an elaborate Turkish bath, indispensable to the middle-eastern proclivities of the master.

Early in January 1924, Gurdjieff arrived on the SS *Paris*. Among the thirty people who accompanied him were Mme Olga de Hartmann, then his secretary, and her husband, Thomas de Hartmann, a gifted pianist and composer who in the old days had played for the Czar and composed music for the Imperial Ballet. It was Hartmann who put Gurdjieff's musical themes into playable script. Later the troupe was moved to more permanent quarters in a three-storey house on the west side of Manhattan. One side housed Gurdjieff and the Hartmanns; on the other lived the younger students.

Practice sessions of Gurdjieff's sacred dances, called more simply 'movements', were begun in a studio belonging to the dancer Rosetta O'Neil, and later at Lesley Hall, not far from the brownstone house. In the manner of the institute, the students swept, scrubbed the hall, and constructed a stage adequate for three rows of dancers. The watchword was working together. Mme de Hartmann was surrounded by women cutting patterns and sewing costumes. Drums and a piano were moved in. For the first private demonstration of the dancing, Orage invited writers, artists, and other interested people. Gurdjieff seemed gratified by their response, and said his group was ready for a more public demonstration.

Orage had already met Alice and Irene Lewisohn, daughters of the philanthropist responsible for the Lewisohn stadium, who owned the Neighborhood Playhouse. After seeing the movements at Lesley Hall, the sisters offered their theater for the first general showing of the sacred dances, which took place early in February 1924.

It would be difficult to exaggerate the unpreparedness of Americans for that first viewing of Gurdjieff's pupils in action. They knew vaguely that the movements were some sort of special dance, coming from ancient Eastern sources. At that moment, innovative dance centered about the Isadora Duncan influence, then considered revolutionary, or, for more classical tastes, there was a growing interest in ballet. Contradictory rumors about the demonstration in Paris reached the ears of those specially concerned with dance as an art form, who realized that this form would have to be regarded in some new way, and were anxious to be among the first to view it.

Lisa Delza, dancer and choreographer, remembers the excitement she felt at hearing from the poet, Hart Crane, that there was to be a performance of the Gurdjieff movements at the Neighborhood Playhouse, which had an *avant-garde* reputation of its own. 'We went with Jean Toomer and Margaret Naumberg,' Miss Delza recalls,

who was then head of the Walden school. Outside the theater, Orage introduced us to Gurdjieff. He was standing at the lobby entrance handing out tickets – you know how he did things. Some he passed by after he looked them over, and others he gave tickets to. He gave them to us and we went in.

Though he did not take part in the dances, Orage talked from the stage to prepare the audience for what they were about to see. Orage said:

> Such gymnastics as these have a double aim. They contain and express a certain form of knowledge and at the same time serve as a means to acquire a harmonious state of being.
>
> The farthest possible limits of one's strength are known through the combination of unnatural movements in the individual gymnastics, which help to obtain certain qualities of sensation, various degrees of concentration, and the requisite directing of thought and the senses.
>
> Thus the ancient sacred dance . . . is a book, as it were, containing definite knowledge.

The program began with the dancers in an almost military order of seven files and three rows, but costumed with quite unmilitary softness. Both men and women wore white tunics over full white trousers gathered at the ankle, much like the Rajput way of dressing, with its yielding responsiveness to bodily motion. The tunics were belted with wide sashes, looped on the left side, in the seven colors of the spectrum, and for the first few movements the dancers stood in the order: red, orange, yellow, green, blue, indigo, violet. Though they remained so for the 'obligatories', their swift movement in complex figures appeared to make the colors change and shift. Someone in the audience said that it seemed like watching white light passed very slowly through a prism and breaking into its spectral order.

Dervish exercises followed, performed by men in Islamic costumes, and then dances of an elusive beauty, based upon symbols associated with the Gurdjieff work. There was a pause, followed by a silence the audience shared, which has since been noted as characteristic of intermissions at such demonstrations. People seemed not to feel like chattering and were attentive the moment Orage returned to the stage to prepare them for the 'stop' exercise.

As soon as the dancer hears the shout to stop, Orage explained, he must 'freeze' and remain motionless until the signal to melt into his more usual posture. There were several explanations for the exercise, he told them. Since the body is made to stop in quite unplanned positions, the dancer cannot help but observe himself in a new situation – between postures, as it were. This was one way to break the vicious circle of his automatism.

But no explanation could wholly prepare either the pupils or the audience for the stop exercise. Those who saw it were electrified. Some reported their reaction as fear. Others were shocked into the vision of a new human possibility. Others reported that the dancers, still frozen in the stop, fell off the stage into the orchestra pit. That did not, of course, actually happen, but the shock of the immediate and complete obedience to the shouted signal dazzled the audience in unforeseen ways.

After an intermission, there was a demonstration of so-called supernatural phenomena, which Gurdjieff classified under three headings: tricks, semi-tricks and authentic phenomena. All three types were given as if genuine, and the audience was left to distinguish among them. Gurdjieff discouraged superstitious belief in unexamined phenomena. During one of his visits to New York, Muriel Draper's son, the dancer Paul, was hit by a Fifth Avenue bus. He was taken to Mt Sinai Hospital, where Mrs Draper was told that though it was dangerous to operate, it was more dangerous not to, and permission was needed to proceed. She asked to allow Gurdjieff to see her son and was refused. She then telephoned Gurdjieff, described the accident, and asked for help. He asked a few pointed questions, which she was able to answer, paused and said that his advice was not to operate. By late evening, the doctors objected vigorously to the mother's trust in Gurdjieff, warning her that Paul would probably die, his condition had deteriorated and he remained unconscious. Again Mrs Draper called Gurdjieff, desperately recounting medical opinion and asking what to do.

'He your son,' Gurdjieff said, 'you must decide.' When she insisted on his opinion, he once more asked certain questions about Paul, he said again, '*You* must decide. But if you ask me, I say not operate.' A few hours later, Paul came to himself.

Before the week was out he was better and soon recovered completely.

One evening when a number of us were together, Muriel, overwhelmingly grateful that Paul had survived, asked Gurdjieff whether this was what he meant by 'genuine phenomena'. 'How can you tell?' he said. 'If it happen once, maybe accident. If it happen many times, then maybe phenomena.'

To most of the onlookers, in spite of Orage's lucid explanations, the idea that dance could be a way of self-study was foreign. In those days, dance was self-expression. The idea of sustained movement as an avenue to self-awareness was difficult to grasp. Moreover – and this was especially puzzling – these dances were obviously not primarily meant to create an aesthetic response. Instead, those watching were given a glimpse of a moment when the dancers were in touch with unaccustomed levels of feeling and thought. The whole purpose of the dance was the experience of immediate awareness.

An audience of newcomers could hardly be blamed for missing this. For the Gurdjieff sacred dance is a very subtle, if at the same time a direct way of making contact with the sources of attention and sharpening the possibility of accurate inner vision. On his first sight of this form of sacred dance, the distinguished Catholic scholar, Jacques Maritain, called it meditation in motion.

For some, it was difficult to accept that the dancers, absorbed in the study of attention, made no effort to be appealing. Orage tried to make clear that theatrical attraction was not part of the discipline of these movements; there was no attempt to lure the audience. But if the spectators watched carefully, they could recognize the changes in state brought about by the movements and the dancers' attentiveness to them. This form of the Gurdjieff teaching could both produce and demonstrate the transition from ideas to inner content.

While Orage was attempting to transmit these elusive concepts, there were moments when Gurdjieff, watching from the wings and more concerned for his students' training than a public approval, would break into Orage's exposition with a shout. For some, this gave a shocking impression of a harsh riding master cracking his whip. They felt the interruption as demeaning to the one who was throwing light for them upon a difficult subject. Later, when asked about this, Orage answered that he was grateful to have been reminded, at the moment of his own involvement to 'Remember yourself, you idiot!'

The number of people who returned night after night to watch and to wonder gave evidence that the dances had awakened questions for which modern thought had few answers. Many began to question their professional and artistic lives. The realization grew that self-expression was not the answer to their profounder needs. What could they learn? they asked. Was there something to learn that the dancers seemed in possession of as they moved unsmilingly, but with great intensity, through the forms of the dance? What was the message of the stop exercise that shook them so much every time they witnessed it? Some said they felt the need for quite another kind of life, one with more and clearer meaning. Others found it difficult to accept that the performers were not professional dancers. Professionals and amateurs alike soon began asking to study these movements, which seemed to offer a new way of being alive.

Later in February Gurdjieff and Orage took the troupe to Boston to perform at Judson Hall. Pianist Carol Robinson, who was in Boston at the time playing with the Boston Symphony Orchestra, went to the demonstration. It was tremendous, she said later: the audience responded warmly. Gurdjieff was in a most informal mood. When he caught a glimpse of Carol Robinson in the audience, he pointed her out announcing that yesterday she had played on the very stage where he now stood. He was deluged with questions from the people who stayed after the performance to learn more. Gurdjieff answered them, calling as usual on Orage to interpret his heavily accented words into more comprehensible English.

Orage's friends at Harvard had arranged a number of meetings of faculty and students, many of whom were interested and open to Orage's exposition of the Gurdjieff teaching. Among others, he went to see an old contributor to the *New Age*, the Anglo-Indian Ananda Coomaraswamy, then keeper of Indian and Mohammedan Art at the Boston Museum of Fine Arts.

Orage was confident that this man, who was giving the Western world its first insight into the beauty of Indian art and the richness of its metaphysical lore, would be eager to hear the ideas of a living master. I can envision disappointment darkening Orage's mobile face, puzzlement clouding his expectant hazel eyes, and his sensitive mouth tightening as he failed to stir Coomaraswamy. Alas, the latter was immovably engrossed in antique art. Like their mutual friend, A. J. Penty, founder of Guild Socialism, Coomaraswamy was concerned only with the restoration of ancient craftsmanship; he had invented the term 'post-industrialism' to describe his hopes.

Once himself a Guild Socialist, Orage was sympathetic to the medieval emphasis on excellence, even felt it to be indispensable. But ever practical, he could not ignore the direction the machine age was taking. His hope as well as his drive was for a new, as yet unimagined, development of skills the machine age would make possible. In a letter about his visit he wrote, 'Coomaraswamy was fast asleep in his work; and had no attention for other worlds than the long dead.' It seems to have been Orage's first blighted hope in the America he expected so much of.

Following the demonstrations of movements at the Neighborhood Playhouse, there was another on 3 March at Carnegie Hall, which from then on was Gurdjieff's favorite theater. More demonstrations followed in Philadephia and Chicago.

Again Orage's role was to translate Gurdjieff's ideas into language the Americans could understand. Although magnetized by Gurdjieff, they found his speech strange and his ideas so new that they required considerably more than a literal translation. Orage, who had so long and so successfully promoted social and political ideas, was now turning his knowledge and gift to the explication of the Gurdjieff ideas.

Before the trip was over, many people were evincing an interest in going further in the work. Gurdjieff had singled out several people whose talents could be useful in the various aspects of his work, and he invited a number of them to return to France with him. Carol Robinson attributes her inclusion to an incident shortly before the day of sailing.

During movements practice one evening she listened with

growing annoyance to the pianist who was improvising entirely in the key of E minor. Unable to bear it any longer, Carol took her turn at the piano, bursting into Stravinsky's 'Firebird', to make her passionate affirmation. When she finished, she saw Gurdjieff's intent look, and soon she was on the list of those sailing with him to France.

'We were all euphoric,' Carol said, 'looking forward to the totally different life Gurdjieff's very presence was promising. Those of us on the lower decks, that is most of us, went eagerly, when we were invited, up to first class.' She described dinners with him on board ship where, as in his Paris apartment, he made a special event of mealtime. In their urgent desire not to miss anything Gurdjieff might say or do, his 'guests' watched him unblinkingly. Sometimes he gave them a 'look', that verified their thought, or a word of particular application to the one addressed. Or he would tell a story, apropos of something said or shown, that threw an immediate light on person and situation. He was, according to Carol, both specific and general, for every personal comment often humorously made, related at once to the human condition. What 'glittered' was the glimpse of an unexpected truth.

'We always returned from a meeting with him jubilant and hopeful,' Carol said. 'It was a very special time.'

For Orage in New York, it was also a jubilant moment. He was to stay on, to attract more people and prepare them for Gurdjieff's anticipated return the next year. From those in New York with Orage come accounts of the meetings he had with them. They often met in small groups, where intimacy allowed them to speak openly of their efforts, their failures, and their moments of surprising insights into their own nature.

Was Orage feeling it so much himself, they wondered, that he often laid stress on the shortness of human life and the need to be aware of the inevitable death of oneself and of others? The general failure of this realization is an aspect of sleep, which he often said was not metaphor but fact. We go about our everyday life in dreams supported by habits which keep us in a state of 'waking sleep'. All this is part of human mechanicalness: not only do our bodies move mechanically, but we feel mechanically and we think mechanically – what can we call our own true perception?

At a polar opposite is our true nature, which is covered by a crust of mechanicalness and therefore has little direct contact with life. To be alive is wonderful, exciting, mysterious, full of possibilities, yet we seem to prefer, almost to accept, the hypnosis of our usual state. Our work was to participate in waking up, in arousing ourselves from this heavy but comfortable sleep and participate in the movement toward consciousness. Then we would see what was before our eyes, indeed all our senses, and be sensitive to the impact of what is, rather than the dream of what ought to be.

This state of waking sleep, he said, was responsible for the partial moments of identifying ourselves with whatever aspect of our psyche was in command, the many, contradictory impulses we called 'I'. We had many 'I's', each one imagining it represented the whole, each with its own habitual associations, supporting habits that had become invisible to us.

His own discovery of the power of sleep had led to miraculous moments of waking up, which transformed his vision of the world. Orage's uplifted state was apparent to his old friends, even those who were not themselves drawn to the Gurdjieff teaching. John Cowper Powys, the brilliant Welsh novelist and poet, who saw Orage in New York when Gurdjieff had just left, wrote a letter to Orage in which he said, among other things, 'You alone of all men of genius I have ever met seem totally to have conquered pride.' This was certainly not Orage's view of himself, but Philip Mairet, who knew him only as editor and who has written an excellent memoir[4] of the man he knew, thinks that such letters give a true portrait of Orage as many saw him then.

1930
Route 2,
Hillsdale, N.Y.

Dear Orage,

Neither my friend P. nor I can get you out of our heads. We have agreed that your visit to us was the greatest event of our winter in Patchin Place. We came to the conclusion that whatever ambiguousness there may be in the nature of your mythology there must be something profoundly right in your own attitude towards it. There's something so 'fixed-up,' so unctuous and conceited about these Indian Swamis and eso- teric teachers, just as there is about Christian Scientists, some- thing that is unilluminating and does not vibrate to the shocks of real life, something that seems to face life through wads of cotton-wool. We go on puzzling ourselves as to exactly what it is that makes your philosophy so different from this; what it is that makes your philosophy so fresh and natural and faltering and troubled as all genuine attitudes to life ought to be, tenuous and almost brittle and with a peculiar sort of humility in it – no! not exactly brittle; but shaky and troubled and insecure – like Nietzsche and Unamuno and Pascal and Heraclitus. The impression you left was what Spengler calls Magian – like something Early Christian or like those early heretics. We got so strongly the feeling that however unsat- isfactory and even to be condemned your gods might be, your attitude towards them was curiously right and full of incidental illumination like that of Jesus to Jehovah. Whatever cult of consciousness yours may be, its effect on your hearers is startling to people as clairvoyant in *certain directions* as my friend P. and I are. You are undoubtedly right in making so much of humility. That organon of research, that plummet into salt seas, that wise serpent-belly, that Taoistic water seeking its level, has not only been neglected by Greeks and Romans but completely neglected, or indeed not known or heard of, by the stupid thick-skinned bastard-idealists of our time. We got the impression of actually and really – don't be angry now! – having entertained a real Saint that day. It was a very queer feeling. As if you had been a person in armour but who was secretly bleeding from wounds invisible. You didn't convert us one inch or one-hundredth part of an inch to your particular gods or ritual or doctrines or master – but you compelled us and still compel us to accept yourself in your present mood as possessed of some extraordinary psychic secret (one great portion of which is this transcendental humility or whatever it may be).

I think we both snatched at some drop of this virtue or aura or emanation and have used it ever since as a test of spiritual values. It is extraordinary. You alone of all men of genius I have ever met seem totally to have conquered pride. And when one thinks how silly such pride has made people; and how it has spoilt their art – like Victor Hugo, like D'Annunzio, like Tolstoy, it seems to me a triumph of true Machiavellianism of the spirit to have burrowed below this great block of Portland cement into wonderful interstices of moonagate and moonstone below.

But I do think the whole thing is in the Daimonic saintliness which you have somehow, by some extraordinary trick, appropriated to yourself. Those 'secrets' you speak of that you would be willing to follow the Devil Himself in order to learn – we must confess – my friend P. and I – to regard as of slight importance compared with this magical effect which 'the humility of the hunt' after them has produced in you and which is, in itself, so we allow ourselves to feel, *a kind of Absolute* and something infinitely superior to any force that started you on such a path or to any tangible 'secrets' that such a path can lead to. It's no good your telling me that Jesus thought Jehovah was as 'good' as He was Himself. We know that Jehovah was better than Jesus! But of course if for Jehovah you put life, it *is* true that any man of exceptional genius like yourself comes much closer to Life by keeping his skin naked so to say (naked in humility) than by twining it round with those flannel swaddling bands Augustus, according to Suetonius, used; or even by wearing the proud armour of Lucifer. This is a woman's letter, my good Lord, as well as a man's, so this particular tone (of handing out bouquets); almost 'maternal'; which would be intolerably impertinent from a lecturer to so formidable a literary and philosophical critic – is natural and harmless (and not impertinent at all or cool or cheeky) *in two of us* uniting our wits. Indeed I guess it will always take the double wit, of a man and a woman combined, to deal with so subtle a Demonic Saint as yourself!

What we secretly feel ourselves is that you will eventually reach a point when you have attained the extreme of humility such as no longer to be in the least danger of Luciferan pride – and at that point, we hold the view . . . Well – let that go . . . . We know nothing really about it. But sometimes out of the mouths of clumsy onlookers – you know? – even a sage can get something . . . . At any rate you certainly made us both think a lot, and as for anything 'fantastic' about it all – we are completely with you there. In the 'fantastic' lies the essence of things.

Well – I must stop. If in the future you not only defy but separate yourself from all outward authority but that of the Daimon in your own being it will only be, I fancy, when this planetary humility of yours that has proved so illuminating has gone the full length of its serpent's tail! And this may not be far off – Life is more than any authority. They are all stepping-stones and jumping-off places.

Well – good luck go with Orage, you certainly won not only our hero-worship but our most anxious love on your behalf, but that must be a common experience to you in your strange passage through the world.

Good luck to you.

JOHN COWPER POWYS

2
Editor

The object of the Leeds Art Club is to affirm the mutual dependence of art and ideas.   A. R. ORAGE

It was our good fortune that Gurdjieff in 1923 selected Orage to work with him, and later for him, in America. Orage's intelligence and stamina had been abundantly demonstrated in his years as editor of the greatly admired English journal, the *New Age*.

Bernard Shaw, who in his brittle way characterized him as a 'desperado of genius', was the first to suggest in 1905 that Orage forsake Leeds, where he was then teaching school, and go to London to try his wings.

From his earliest school days, Orage was passionately interested in learning and in the meaning of life, and was critical of his own failures of perception. Once early in our acquaintance when someone remarked on the breadth and richness of his mind, Orage replied that on the contrary he had long remarked its faults. On one occasion, when as a schoolboy his teacher asked him to name all the capes between two cities in England, to the amazement of his classmates he took the long way round the island. 'Why didn't it occur to me to take the short way round?' he asked us. In other ways, he was grateful to have started his schooling in a country school, where he felt one met all human types and learned early to know instinctively the faults and virtues of one's fellows.

Later, when educating others became his profession, self-education retained its priority. Nothing fascinated him more than pursuing wisdom Socratic fashion and listening to the discoveries of fellow questioners. It is not surprising that soon after his arrival at Leeds, he joined a Plato group. Before long, he was a favorite lecturer whom many, including Shaw, came to hear. Philip Mairet describes that period glowingly:[1]

> Never was his voice so magnetic as in his brilliant discourses at this period. . . . The lucidity and logical sequence of his thought was fortified by an enthusiastic conviction that held his listeners spellbound. He seemed not only a servant of truth but its lover – as indeed he was: it was the secret of his pre-eminence in discussion.

But the young Orage aspired to a larger audience, and together with his friend, Holbrook Jackson, began in the spring of 1907 to negotiate for a moribund sectarian paper called the *New Age*. Neither of them had even the small amount of money it required. Shaw contributed £500 and another admirer of Orage, who insisted on anonymity, gave them the same amount. Much later it was learned that the latter was Alexander Wallace, who in time wrote for the *New Age* under the pseudonym of M. B. Oxon.

From the start the journal was a *succès d'estime*. Bernard Shaw may have hoped that his favorite brand of socialism, called Fabian[2], would be its focal point, but Orage made it clear that the journal would not limit itself to any one economic theory. According to Mairet, Holbrook Jackson was an eclectic socialist. Orage defined his own views in these words:

> My brand of socialism was a blend, or, let us say, an anthology of all these (referring here to many other theories, not all of them economic), to which from my personal predilections and experience I add a good practical knowledge of the working classes.

Before long, the *New Age* became Orage's sole responsibility, and was soon known throughout England and in America for its high literary quality. Roger Lipsey calls Orage 'a man of faultless literary taste. . . . By 1911 it [the *New Age*] had become a leading socialist commentator, appreciated for its literary and journalistic quality outside socialist circles.'[3]

The best minds in Britain counted it an honor to have their poems, stories, essays and articles appear in its discriminating pages. Among them were Arnold Bennett, G. K. Chesterton, T. S. Eliot, W. D. Howells, Ezra Pound and, of course, Shaw himself. What is more, Orage's gift for recognizing talent in the germ brought him writers then unknown who later became skilled and finished artists such as Edwin Muir, Sir Herbert Read, Ruth Pitter and Katherine Mansfield.

In a 1978 BBC broadcast, 'The Eye of the Storm', Lesley Montgomery says of Orage, 'In the anonymous role of editor, he was to prove a sounding board for most of the exciting ideas of the early years of this century.'

Storm Jameson, in describing her early struggles as a writer, tells of her joy at getting a piece into the *New Age:*[4]

That paper was the Bible of our generation. We would rather go hungry than not buy it. We quoted it, argued with it, and formed ourselves on it. I suppose that Mr. A. R. Orage had a sharper influence on the young men of our day than any other man.

In America Orage had many readers and admirers, including the *New Republic's* distinguished editor, Herbert Croly, and the joint editors of the *Little Review* (first publishers of James Joyce), Margaret Anderson and Jane Heap. Among the young intelligentsia in the American universities there were many who read the *New Age* regularly.

Long before meeting Gurdjieff, Orage had been searching for a path to 'objective' self-knowledge. At the core of his study of literature was the question of life's ultimate meaning. When still young, he became an ardent student of Indian metaphysics and scripture, particularly of the *Mahabharata*. His knowledge of Eastern teachings ranged beyond the imagination of most of us.

As early as 1907, he wrote a small book entitled *Consciousness: Animal, Human and Superman*, raising questions he would take up with Gurdjieff fifteen years later. 'Human consciousness,' he says,[5]

> is no less and no more than the prenatal state of a being who shall compare with man, not as man compares with the animal (for man is only a higher animal) but as the animal compares with the vegetable kingdom. For I believe that the only difference between man and the animals is that man is the most pregnant animal, in whom is taking place the birth, not of a being like himself, but of an infinitely superior being altogether.

His use of the word 'superman' in the title reflects his study of Nietzsche, a strange choice in retrospect until one reads his two excellent introductory books,[6] which make plain Orage's concern with freeing western thought of its arid approach to consciousness and morality, and letting the winds of revolutionary ideas blow through the prevailing culture. The ideas Orage selects and interprets are a key to his interest. Man is a bridge, he would quote. For though he expounded Nietzsche's Dionysian spirit, there is no doubt that Orage himself was Apollonian. That accounts for his attraction to the Plato Group in association with the professors at the University of Leeds and, according to Mairet, Orage had so acute a critical sense that he was saved from the sentimentality Mairet regards as a common danger of long service to Platonism. This may be what led him around 1905 to join the Theosophical Society, where his interest in Indian philosophy was fed, and where he became a Society lecturer. Mairet also says, 'He taught with a critical spirit and a ruthless analysis that seemed to call everything into question and even threaten danger to their own most cherished ideas. They wished he would be less "destructive".'[7]

Before long, he and other members objected to the continued membership, as well as the influence, of Charles Leadbeater. Mrs Annie Besant, then head of the Society, refused to expel or demote her favorite. Orage decried Leadbeater's influence on the younger members because of his emphasis on psychic phenomena: impressionable young people could be lost forever in the psychic domain. Orage was in search of someone wise, not one who could astound with supernatural tricks. Moreover, by then he had grown tired of hearing provincial attitudes expressed toward his own skeptical views.

At this same time, in Russia, another man in search of a teacher or a school was the mathematician and journalist, P. D. Ouspensky. Like Orage, his quest had led him to the Theosophical Society, where he studied Mme Blavatsky's writings. Unsatisfied, he continued his search for a more direct and unequivocal approach to the hidden knowledge he felt sure existed. Where would it still be taught? What part of the world would have these schools? Some, he reasoned, were most likely to exist in India or Ceylon, or perhaps Egypt. And shortly thereafter he was to set out on a journey to those countries in search of the miraculous.

Before starting out he visited London. There he met Orage. They talked about their common interest in metaphysical teachings, and their belief that esoteric schools still existed. Before he left London, Ouspensky promised Orage he would send him accounts of his travels. This was not to be. The account of his journey would appear much later in *A New Model of the Universe*, published in 1931.[8] Ouspensky's lectures on the subject in Moscow and St Petersburg, chiefly in 1915, were attended by large audiences.

Before the two men met again it was 1914, and World War I had begun. On his return from the East, Ouspensky again visited London, promising Orage some essays and articles. He then made his way back to Russia by way of Norway, Sweden and Finland, arriving in St Petersburg, already re-named Petrograd, in November 1914. Six months later, in the midst of a war soon to turn to revolution, he met the man he was to acknowledge as his teacher: George Ivanovitch Gurdjieff.

As late as 1919, Orage was unaware that his friend, Ouspensky, had found someone who 'knew'. What came instead from him were vivid accounts of life in Bolshevik Russia, which Orage published in the *New Age*, while revolution was going on. On 25 July 1919, Ouspensky wrote from Ekaterinodar:

It is now two years since I last saw [a copy of] the *New Age*, and I do not know what is being said and thought and written in England and what you know. I can only guess. During this period we here have lived through so many marvels that I honestly pity everybody who has not been here, everybody who is living in the old way, everybody who is ignorant of what we now know. . . .

Everything leads to results that are contrary to what people intend to bring about and towards which they strive. . . . The people who are now struggling to bring about the re-creation of a great, united, indivisible, and so on, Russia are gathering results very little resembling what they are striving for.

No lover of the Bolsheviks, Ouspensky credits them with a better purpose than they were in fact achieving. 'The Bolsheviks did not propose to live in a state of perpetual war and to introduce into Russia what is in actual fact the dictatorship of the criminal element.' Nevertheless, that is how things turned out.

For a time at least, some communication between England and Russia was possible. Ouspensky addressed to Orage, and to his many English readers, an account of what was happening to prices as compared with the money one could earn:

You will ask how it is possible to live under such conditions. And this is the most occult aspect of the whole question. I will answer for myself: I personally am still alive only because my boots and my trousers and other articles of clothing – all 'old campaigners' – are still holding together. When they end their existence, I shall evidently end mine.

Orage wrote at once to F. S. Pinder, the British Government representative in Ekaterinodar, who put Ouspensky on his staff. Stanley Nott, a pupil of Gurdjieff years later, speculates as to whether Pinder paid him out of his own pocket.

By December of that same year, Ouspensky wrote that he was deeply troubled about what was going on:

My bewildered and hungry country; where people are thrown out of railway carriages; where every conception of cultural values is gone; where intellectual life has ceased long ago; where the number of people under the command of somebody or other is continually increasing. And the sole aim of these commanding persons is to improve their own position at the expense of those who are deprived of all rights.

Bolshevism is a poisonous plant.

Alive to every idea that promised light on his inquiry into the nature of man, Orage had been in 1912 the first in England to publish Freud in a non-professional journal – a good year before the first English translation of *The Interpretation of Dreams*. When Dr Eder read a paper on Freud before the neurological section of the British Medical Association, the chairman and the entire audience rose and stalked out without a word at the end of his talk.[9] Clearly, the subject of psychoanalysis was forbidden territory. None the less, at Orage's suggestion, a group of young London intellectuals met to study the Freudian hypothesis – among them such men as Dr James D. Young; J. M. Alcock; Dr M. D. Eder; Dr Maurice Nicoll (a Jungian); the novelist, J. D. Beresford; Rowland Kenny, editor of the *Daily Herald* and Clifford Sharp of the *New Statesman*. (Some of them later became students of the Gurdjieff ideas, of whom Dr Nicoll is an outstanding example.) After some months of intense study, they agreed that what was now needed was 'psycho-synthesis',[10] which was Orage's term.

Ouspensky's own adventures during those years led him far from Freud and 'defective' reasoning.[11] For in spite of the changes taking place in Russian life, and the risks for all professional people of remaining in Russia, Ouspensky stayed with Gurdjieff, or close to him, for at least five years. For a direct and singularly well-remembered picture of the life and teaching during those years, the book to read is Ouspensky's *In Search of the Miraculous*.[12] Many of Orage's students heard this read in manuscript, though it was not published until after Ouspensky's death.

From his letters in the *New Age* during the war years, it

would be difficult to divine that new and wondrous things had entered Ouspensky's life: he was studying the Gurdjieff teaching with considerably more of himself than the intellect; his book *Tertium Organum* (The Third Canon of Thought)[13] was being read by every Russian who could get hold of it; and to each of his lectures on his travels in India a thousand listeners crowded into St Petersburg's Alexandrovsky Hall.

As early as 1918, Nicholas Bessaraboff, a young Russian who had managed to get out of Russia, took *Tertium Organum* to Claude Bragdon, the well-known American architect and author, whose book *Four-Dimensional Vistas*[14] marked him as the perfect fellow-translator. By December 1919 the two men completed the translation, and in 1920 it was published by the Manas Press.

How to reach Ouspensky himself was the question. Dhan Gopal Mukerji[15] told the translators that a series of Ouspensky's letters were appearing in the *New Age*. Orage put Bragdon and Bessaraboff in touch with Ouspensky, who by then had taken refuge with his wife and family in Constantinople. He responded by asking for help to get them all to England or America. Orage and Bragdon both appealed to Lady Rothermere, who admired Ouspensky's writings, and she came to the rescue, generously financing their journey to London. Thus her beneficence made possible Orage's introduction to the work of G. I. Gurdjieff.

3
Kitchen boy

Literature at best is only a perfect substitute for a perfect reality.

A. R. ORAGE

In the spring of 1921 a letter from Ouspensky announced that he was coming to London to live, and was now ready to speak about the 'fragments of an unknown teaching'. This was the first indication to Orage that Ouspensky had found what they were both seeking.

Jubilant, Orage gathered together his band of psychological investigators to hear Ouspensky's message. Rowland Kenny, who was present at their first meeting, relates an incident characteristic of Ouspensky and Orage as I later knew them. Concerned that his friends listen carefully to the new material, Orage spoke emphatically about the need for a re-evaluation of psychological principles. Often, he said, people needed preparation in order to hear something genuinely new. Ouspensky interrupted him. 'Why waste time, Orage? Tell Kenny what we are meeting for.'

At this Ouspenskian tempo the group met weekly in Lady Rothermere's study in St John's Wood. Before long, other London intellectuals came to listen, participate, or simply to visit and observe. Among them were T. S. Eliot, a close friend of Orage; David Garnett; Sir Herbert Read; Aldous Huxley and Gerald Heard.

A letter to Claude Bragdon dated 30 May 1922, gives a vivid picture of the enthusiastic reception of Ouspensky's first lectures in London:[1]

I had the satisfaction of showing your letter to both Mr.

Ouspensky and to Lady Rothermere, both of whom are my very good friends as well as yours. Ever since Mr. Ouspensky came to London under Lady Rothermere's auspices last August, I have been attending his lectures, and more and more and still more I find myself absorbing his teaching . . . Mr. Ouspensky is the first teacher I have met who has impressed me with ever-increasing certainty that he knows and can do. Lady Rothermere is exceedingly interested also, and I much hope she will be able to continue, for she has many gifts. I am sure you would be delighted to share in his work. In the meantime, I thank you with cordial greetings for your praise of my *Readers and Writers* and for the gift of the two books. I shall treasure them in the hope of one day seeing you in person to discuss these with you. With kind regards. Yours sincerely,   A. R. Orage

Many years later Orage said that when he listened to the Gurdjieff-inspired Ouspensky he felt like a medieval alchemist in search of gold. But when Gurdjieff himself visited the group in London one cold February evening in 1922, he felt that he had at last found the gold itself.

Gurdjieff had established his Institute for the Harmonious Development of Man in the town of Avon, near Fontainebleau, in France. The property with enough land for a kitchen garden, a small wood and a spacious seventeenth-century house, had once been inhabited by monks and was still called the Prieuré (priory). It was said that Mme de Maintenon had lived there, and that an underground passageway led to the palace at Fontainebleau.

Ouspensky told me that he had watched Orage unseen from the window of his flat in London one autumn day in 1922 when Orage came to see him. He saw by Orage's face that he had decided to go to work directly with Gurdjieff in France. On entering the study, as he began in his courteous way to ask Ouspensky's opinion, he was not permitted to finish his sentence. 'I can see that you have already made up your mind,' said Ouspensky, 'so why ask me?'

In other moods, Ouspensky had an old-world charm characteristic of the cultivated Russians of his time, with warmth as well as wit, that those of us who admired and respected him were grateful for. But when in a self-disciplinary mood, he never said more than he thought necessary, even when it hindered clarification to be so terse.

In this instance, Ouspensky had to accept that Orage reccognized in Gurdjieff the key to his long search, just as Ouspensky himself had seven years earlier. At fifty, with little more than a decade to live, Orage was convinced that he had at last found a true teacher. Thus it was that in October 1922, Orage gave up his post as editor of the *New Age* and departed from the forefront of the intellectual life of London to take part in Gurdjieff's work at the Prieuré.

His sudden move startled those closest to him, for Orage was not a man who talked about his problems. He would have thought and suffered, tried experiments to test himself, and then, at a certain point, have said, 'This is what I am going to do.' Among those stunned by his decision was his faithful secretary and manager, Alice Marks, who could not understand his abandonment of the journal in which she had for ten years been a devoted partner. When she finally brought herself to ask for an explanation of his leaving, he replied simply, 'I am going to find God.'

On his arrival at the Prieuré Orage's period of testing began. Rumors reached his friends that the celebrated editor, now kitchen boy, was cheerfully scrubbing pots and dumping garbage. Others reported the fastidious Orage mopping latrines and laboring in field and garden. It is not unlikely that digging, raking and hoeing cost something in physical suffering at first, not to mention the inevitable boredom of repetitive chores. But Orage had begun life as a Yorkshire country boy and was familiar with the rigors of farm work.

Bells were rung to announce the daily schedule. There was the 'little' bell, at six in the morning, calling the entire household to a meager breakfast of coffee and bread. After the quickly consumed meal, the men and women hurried to their tasks: farm work, preparing meals, housework, laundry, and for some, special assignments given by Gurdjieff for a specific teaching purpose.

In the evening, having 'paid for their existence' people dropped their daytime roles, scrubbed, changed, and, summoned by the 'big bell', assembled for dinner, often quite sumptuosly prepared. Afterwards, they moved to the drawing room to await what Gurdjieff had in store for them. Often he began by speaking of one or another aspect of their inner work, such as the effort to become more aware of the part played in their lives by violence, envy and fear. Or about self-remembering and the approach to a more aware state. He would unexpectedly point out a particular stupidity, sometimes in general and sometimes singling out this one's swagger and that one's false humility.

At times he gave exercises for the head, the heart and the body, to awaken an experience of balance in the organism. Some were to be carried out during the daily chores, and always the struggle was towards awareness, the *raison d'être* of the Institute.

For many, the high point of the evening came with the Gurdjieff movements, in which everyone, whether talented for the dance or totally awkward, participated. These 'Sacred Gymnastic' forms, practised under the vaulting roof of the rug-strewn 'Study House', moved in intricate patterns accompanied by near-Eastern melodic rhythms and fragments of Temple Dances. These Gurdjieff had hummed into the ear of Thomas de Hartmann, one-time darling of the Czar's Conservatory, who then transformed them into magical music.

A Russian woman, then in her early twenties, described ruefully the fruits of daily tasks at the Prieuré, which found her milking the cows at five in the morning and again at nightfall. By evening her body asked only for sleep. She would struggle with fatigue, lifting her heavy eyelids, hoping to respond to the promise of a special reading or direct instruction for 'those who are still awake'. More often than not, she confessed, real sleep, bodily sleep, took over.

Rumors about Orage's life at the Prieuré were beginning to be bruited about. Worried by Orage's letters, his close friend,

Professor Denis Saurat, went there to see him in February 1923. Saurat could not but deplore the fact that 'Orage, a powerful person in the English literary world, who could have become the greatest critic of English literature, had sold the *New Age*'. He describes Orage as a surprise at first sight:[2]

When I knew him he was almost obese, carrying some ninety-five kilos of flesh on a huge, bony frame. But coming toward me was a thin, almost emaciated Orage with a troubled face. An Orage who seemed larger, whose movements were quicker and stronger; in better health, but not happy.

Orage answered my questions about his health and the physical change in him by telling me something of his life. He went to bed at midnight or later, was on his feet around 4 A. M. and to work: hard work in the Prieuré park where digging and building were going on. Hurried meals, quickly eaten. From time to time, he joined the others in group gymnastics in the presence of the master. Then, once more, ditches to dig or fill in. 'Sometimes Gurdjieff had us spend a whole day digging an enormous ditch in the park, then he would have us spend the following day putting back into the ditch and heaping up what we had taken out the day before.'

'Gurdjieff keeps us always occupied. The soul can develop only if the body is in perfect balance. We are taught to master our muscles: we know how to do the roughest work and we also know how to move the left arm in a different rhythm from the right arm: to beat in four-four time with the right arm and simultaneously, with the left arm, in three-four time.'

Of difficulties there were no doubt scores. Stanley Nott reports Orage as saying:[3]

When I was in the depths of despair, feeling that I could go on no longer, I vowed to make extra effort, and just then something changed in me. Soon, I began to enjoy the hard labour, and a week later, Gurdjieff came to me and said,

'Now, Orage, I think you dig enough. Let us go to the café and drink coffee.' From that moment things began to change.

To those of us in New York, Orage reminisced about the hungry intellectuals playing hooky to walk to the village bakery, smacking their lips at the vision of sweets. Meeting a fellow worker triumphantly munching the next to last cream puff, they raced each other as if to pluck the golden apple of wisdom.

In general, Orage's old friends, though insisting that his present life did not suit his talents, agreed that he looked well, that his intelligence was, if anything, sharpened. And, as always, he was loved and admired by his fellow aspirants – Russian, English and the few French.

During his visit, Saurat succeeded in interviewing Gurdjieff, finding him courteous, responsive to all questions, and leaving his visitor with a strong impression of Gurdjieff's profound knowledge. However, it was many years later, after the publication of Gurdjieff's *Beelzebub's Tales to his Grandson*,[4] that Saurat acknowledged the greatness of Gurdjieff's philosophy and 'method'. He said then that he understood well why Orage in 1923 had accepted the discipline of obedience.

Early in December 1923, the emotional climate at the Institute began to heat up. There was soon to be a movements demonstration in Paris – the first of its kind. Much of Gurdjieff's time was given to rehearsals, with something new always added. Work on costumes went on, lighting, at which Alexandre de Salzmann was an acknowledged artist, and the many details such an exhibition would demand.

The first public demonstration at the Champs Elysées Theater on 13 December 1923, was greeted with mixed reactions. To some viewers, it was a startlingly new, *avant-garde* presentation of dance forms based on inner experience. To others, the exercises had no aesthetic value, and were marred by the imposition of a discipline that bore no relation to the beauty of dance.

Orage, who had taken part in the practices, was not among the performers. For Gurdjieff, having studied him closely during his many months at the Prieuré, chose him to go to the United

States as the first representative there of Gurdjieff's work. Orage never revealed the substance of his many conversations with Gurdjieff in preparation for this undertaking. He was on his way to New York, accompanied by a Russian pupil of Gurdjieff's, Dr Stjoernval. Their assignment, and specifically Orage's task, was to attract from among the intelligentsia men and women who would be open to the radical world-view Gurdjieff was about to bring to America. Thus Orage was to take the first step in establishing there the Gurdjieff teaching.

4
Inner fires

Objective knowledge is truth. Truth is at the bottom of the well.

A. R. ORAGE

In fact, as well as in reputation, Orage had what was necessary for the delicate task of inducing critical people to listen, to question and to think. However, it was his reputation as the editor of the *New Age*, knowledgeable in the fields of economics, psychology and, most of all, in literature, that drew many who might otherwise have been reluctant to give metaphysical ideas a hearing.

It was a moment when he had to use all the ingenuity he possessed to attract suitable people. For the intellectual world was then magnetized either with universal salvation by the redistribution of wealth according to Karl Marx, or with saving individuals one at a time, hour by hour, as promised by Sigmund Freud.

Many were pious Marxists who judged people and events solely in terms of the class struggle, with an orthodoxy even more rigid than we know today. For them, no human motivation other than the economic existed, and their minds were closed to men's non-material needs; the human dilemma required no further thought, only revolutionary action of the kind they advocated. Among conscientious liberals, many seemed blind to the inquisitional realities of the emerging Communist regimes. They refused categorically to admit that millions of Russian farmers and workers were being regimented and brutally murdered for the new version of 'pie in the sky.' To naive liberals, the need to understand the meaning of one's life was religious nonsense and, as all right-thinking people knew, religion was the opium of the masses.

Freudians were equally ardent. They regarded concern with the meaning of life as 'neurotic', rooted in repressed sexual impulses and flummoxed toilet training. And so it went with the advocates of other popular theories. (This is not to say that Freud, Adler, Watson and the rest must be held accountable for half-digested, seminal ideas regurgitated and misapplied by their loquacious adepts.)

Such psychological schools considered themselves branches of natural science, the main tree of knowledge. Scientific investigators, however, often rejected their hypotheses as not measurable, and therefore not valid. That is to say, other ways of testing the subtler manifestations of life were not yet accepted as legitimate. Here and there a few scientists were querying the metaphysical foundations of scientific thought, though for the most part people were living in what René Guénon has termed the 'reign of quantity'. Only a man as aware of scientific thinking and as rational as Orage could attract to lectures of the Gurdjieff ideas critical practitioners of the sciences, mathematics, the arts, architecture, poetry, letters, ballet and the law.

Among them were Melville Cane, the lawyer poet; Lincoln Kirstein, editor of *Hound & Horn*; John O'Hara Cosgrave, Sunday editor of the *New York World*; Hugh Ferriss, architectural artist of the burgeoning skyline of Manhattan; Mabel Dodge Luhan and her Indian husband, Tony; Gorham Munson, critic and professor of literature; T. S. Matthews of the *New Republic* and for many years after, managing editor of *Time*; Jean Toomer, the black author of *Cane*; C. Daly King, writer and psychologist; painter Boardman Robinson; mathematician, John Riordan; museum curator, Carl Zigrosser; and such distinguished members of the legal profession as Reese Alsop, Allan Brown and Amos Pinchot.

If Orage's reputation drew people to hear his introduction to the Gurdjieff ideas, it was the lucidity of his interpretations that kept them returning to meetings. Editor Margaret Anderson sums up the part played by Orage:[1]

For myself I know that, without Orage's grasp of the Gurdjieff ideas, and his manner of elucidation, I might never have
understood enough of them to have investigated further. I
can think of no other approach that would have completely
held my attention.

In his biography, Claude Bragdon, architect and author of many
books, including one on the Fourth Dimension, and translator
of *Tertium Organum*, had this to say:[2]

It was Orage, the perfect disciple, the Plato to this Socrates,
who was responsible for most of the success which attended
the movement in America. His charming manner and brilliant
mind did much to counteract the bewilderment in which
Gurdjieff so often left his auditors.

C. Daly King in his privately published book, *The Oragean
Version*, tells a story that was true for many people who had
seen the movements demonstration. He had been touched and
interested but had returned to his own preoccupation with psychology and Egyptology. He credits Jessie Dwight with having
been persistent enough to get him to a lecture of Orage's, and
remembers the meeting-place as some sort of private school. It
was most likely the Walden School. King says that what impressed him most was the utter rationality of what he heard.[3]

Perhaps I had gone in the expectation of a proselytizing ha-
rangue; and certainly I had taken with me an incredulous
attitude, prone to raise objection to everything put forward.
My incredulity was not admitted; instead, it was demanded
that I adopt scepticism toward what I heard, i.e., that I should
neither believe nor disbelieve.

In 1927, under a pseudonym, King wrote a book which sought
to show the relation between scientific psychology and the
Gurdjieff teaching.[4]

All the spring of 1924 and into the early summer Orage
continued with his exposition of the Gurdjieff ideas. What fas-

cinated King and many others who were beginning to find the groups essential to their lives, was not alone Orage's brilliant exposition. It was much more the way he was toward the people who came. His personal interest in every member was extraordinary. Each person existed for him as an individual; he never swept up their problems in metaphysical generalizations. At the same time, he could put them into a large, more inclusive perspective that made it possible to take a fresh look and not drown in one's subjectivity.

Mavis McIntosh recalls one such characteristic moment:

It was cold in January 1926 in New York: dry with a penetrating wind, and at night the chill factor seemed to rise painfully. I left a meeting that had been held in an apartment far uptown and hurried to the nearest Fifth Avenue bus stop, eager for the long, warm ride to my room in the Village. Orage was suddenly there beside me, hat pulled down against the wind, plaid wool scarf wrapped around his neck. His coat, like mine, seemed thin, but he didn't shiver as I did. A bus appeared and we hopped on, but as I turned to find a seat inside Orage pulled my arm and pushed me up the stairs to the open top deck. He couldn't want to sit there and freeze! But he did. He slapped my back and shoulders and laughed at my miserable huddling. 'Come on,' he said, *'feel* the cold – and build a little fire! You know, there are lamas in Tibet who can sit naked in the snow feeling as warm as toast! They build an inner fire, and it isn't just a trick. That's what our work is, I think – to build an inner fire, starting with the small spark we know is there. Yes, that is what I must do . . .' His voice was soft; for a moment I was warm.

From notes taken at that time, Orage's imagery must often have produced sudden delighted recognition from his listeners. On one occasion when the members were trying to pin down 'self-observation', he recalled a man in London who thought he was interested in knowing himself, but was chiefly concerned with note-taking. 'He went from Ouspensky's large group to his own little one,' Orage said, 'peddling his notes.' He paused for a moment, smiled, and cherubically invoked the ancient Oriental metaphor. 'He was an ass, carrying the mysteries.'

'Could physical or organic changes take place as a result of the self-observation we are trying?' a member queried. This could happen, Orage granted. 'But,' he added, 'there is no cause for alarm. This work can harm only two classes of experimenter: those who work, or think they do, on communication with the dead, and those who undertake artificial breathing.'

That rang the alarm bell for the frequenters of psychic seances. But about this Orage was firm. Making a practice of trying so-called spirit communication indicated a pathological state. Although the Gurdjieff teaching attracted serious people, there was inevitably a lunatic figure which could distort the light of the highest star into the murkiness of moonshine. When one woman insisted that she knew an extraordinary medium who wanted to come to one of the meetings, Orage was patient but final in his refusal.

His attitude toward fascination with psychic phenomena came from his years of observation of the harmful effects, from his point of view, of attachment to the psychic domain. He believed it stood in the way of genuine inner growth, and his intention, or his hope, was to arrive himself, and help other people to arrive at objective conscience as taught by Gurdjieff.

As the meetings went on, Orage tried to evoke questions about 'work' difficulties, in order to clarify efforts and put the results into some realizable order. An increasing interest in the duration of a 'conscious' effort began. Much was asked about the separation of 'I', the power of attention, from 'it', the self this attention was focusing on: the observer and the observed.

Here Orage's imagery was a great help. Agreeing that by now many of us had probably had seconds of consciousness, he called them 'winks of wakefulness'. 'We should know what it is to be winkingly awake,' he said,

but we ought not yet to expect more. Is there anyone who can now sustain the waking state for more than five minutes? Five minutes is not a long time, but the organism remembers and records, like a dictaphone. Later, the 'I' can go over what the organism has recorded.

As an exercise to help us he suggested that before going to sleep we try to remember how we began the day, and move through it, as we might watch a film, to the very end.

'First we have to learn how to get into the right state of attention. Each exercise makes the next one possible through the energy created by the preceding one.'

Many of these first students were, of course, familiar with psychoanalytic terms – some were veterans of the Freudian couch – and, in general, thought that self-observation was some form of analysis. They had to struggle with the distinction between the two, and try to understand Orage's insistence upon the difference between the haunting memories of introspection, on the one hand, and, on the other hand, the rigor of seeing, in the very midst of emotional turmoil, how it is now rather than how it may once have begun.

In those early days, Orage expressed very simply the effort of self-observation.

Be aware of your behavior at the time of its occurrence. The conditions are simple but difficult. Observe without criticism, without trying to change anything, without tutorialness, without analysis, without identification, with all of your perceptions, without concern for the time or place.

Orage never tired of saying that work on oneself began with this instruction. It existed in a number of stages, but we must begin with the first stage, itself no easy matter since the direct knowledge of oneself depended upon the appropriate state, and it was difficult to reach it.

As people reported on their experiences, it sometimes seemed as though no example was accepted as non-identified observation. Each time, however, Orage said plainly why this was so: the very concern to succeed often stood in the way. A physician gave as an example an account of observing himself during a treatment. His anxiety for the patient stood in the way of complete objectivity. To the degree that he 'saw' his anxiety, he felt he had observed more truly.

It was difficult – or rather, next to impossible – as many reported, to be active when the ego was touched to the quick, and to watch at the same time. Much of the response was a cry for help or an account of efforts gone awry. At that same meeting, Orage gave the story of a surgeon who arrived at non-identification when he had unexpectedly to operate on his own son. While operating, his state was extraordinarily clear. It was as though he had abandoned his egotistic fear and put his skill at the service of a more intelligent force in himself. He continued to the end of a two-hour long surgery, and one could call this, Orage said, 'objective prayer', about which we know very little.

In summing up before the groups disbanded for the summer what the last six months had achieved, Orage was generally pleased. The people he had attracted to the work were by now not only drawn to the study of the Gurdjieff ideas, but had begun to try to apply them in their own lives.

An aspect of his responsibility to Gurdjieff, which had not occurred to Orage in advance, was the task to attract money. The whole of Gurdjieff's entourage, spending their entire time carrying out Gurdjieff's instructions and with emigrés' pocket books, had to be supported. It was obvious enough that Gurdjieff took very little for himself and always shared what he received, lavishly or frugally, depending on the amount at any time available. There was also the fact of human nature that Gurdjieff often referred to: people will only value what they pay for, in all ways, including financial.

The need for money was met by some who could well afford it and by many others who gave their utmost, which was not much. Added together, their contributions made it possible for Gurdjieff and his party to stay in America a few months. Orage had struggled with his disinclination to ask for money, and now could send a considerable sum to Gurdjieff for the needs of the Institute.

No doubt, with one side of his nature, Orage missed his journalist life and friends in London. But he found himself very sympathetic to Americans and responsive to their eagerness for his friendship. Though still a 'seeker' after truth, he felt nourished, and he was feeding others. Soon he would see Gurdjieff again, and would receive the material he needed to continue as the American representative of the Work.

5
Cultivating the garden

Meanwhile, the garden must be cultivated, though I do not know, I only feel the necessity. And I can see no better patch, save ourselves individually, to work upon than the community in which we happen to live.   A. R. ORAGE

Suddenly in July 1924 Orage was shocked by the news that Gurdjieff had been seriously injured in a motor accident. There were even doubts he would recover. Around him at the Prieuré, the people were dazed.

There have been many versions of the accident, though for the most part they agree on the main points. Olga de Hartmann, then his secretary, has said that although Gurdjieff almost in-variably took people with him when he drove, on that day he made a deliberate exception. She had been with him in Paris, but even though she asked specially to drive back with him on that hot July day rather than return to Fontainebleau by train, he insisted on going alone.

According to the de Hartmanns,[1] Gurdjieff told her that the steering wheel of his car had been giving trouble. She then ordered the garage mechanic to give the car a thorough going-over before Gurdjieff picked it up later in the day. So it may have been, as Mme de Hartmann believed, that the damaged steering wheel, inadequately repaired, was the cause of the accident.

There is also the unexplained fact that although Gurdjieff was unconscious when found, he had somehow dragged himself out of the car, or been lifted out, and lay on the grass with his head on a car cushion.

In New York, a week or more before the accident, the poet Jean Toomer had received permission to visit the Prieuré. He arrived a week after Gurdjieff's accident, but wholly ignorant of it. He was given a room on the 'Monks' Corridor', the third floor of the lovely old château, and began to take part in the general work.

It was several days before he found an explanation for the heavy atmosphere he had met on his arrival. Like many others, Toomer could not readily believe that a man of Gurdjieff's special abilities would fail to defend himself against accident. But the *fact*, as Toomer says, had to be faced. Many years later, he wrote that he had found the people at the Prieuré with no unity among them, walled off from each other, some depressed, some melancholy, some very uncertain as to the future, some carrying on efficiently.

'With the forced withdrawal of Mr. Gurdjieff's active presence, the work of the Institute had come to a halt. So had the spirit. Le Prieuré, as an estate, had to be maintained.'[2]

Across the Atlantic, Orage was having to deal with the problem of that maintenance, his own sense of imminent loss, and that of the people under his guidance. Immediate and vital was the need for still more money to keep the Prieuré going and to look after the 'parasites', as Gurdjieff with ironic affection called its inhabitants. But most of all, there must be provision for the desperately ill Gurdjieff.

According to Mme de Hartmann, the doctors regarded Gurdjieff's condition as critical. Though no bones were broken, nor was the skull fractured, the concussion appeared to be severe. For five days he seemed totally unconscious, and the anxiety about him brought an intense seriousness to the working groups.

The concern Orage felt for what he now saw as his primary obligation cannot be exaggerated. He was to say later that this was a critical step in his own comprehension of the full meaning of responsibility. Those who worked with him during that period recall that his determination to provide the resources seemed almost an obsession. Money making had never been Orage's preoccupation, to say the least, in spite of his having been born and brought up in poverty. As a Grub Street journalist, he was used to stretching what shillings and pence came his way to support the *New Age* and its enterprises. He had long since accepted that in our economic world, living from hand to mouth was the usual condition of those who give their best energy to the search for understanding. Contributors to his journal, as well as he as editor, worked for rewards other than money.

But now Gurdjieff's future and that of his work were threatened. Later Orage remarked a number of times that all his life he had been naive about money, even for less sacred undertakings, and now perforce he was learning.

In France, those closest to Gurdjieff were doing what they could. There are touching accounts of the Russian emigrés who sold or pawned their jewelry, or whatever else was pawnable. Some who could hardly speak French were trying outside jobs whenever they could find them. Yet much more than could be readily collected in that way was needed. As Toomer noted, the Prieuré had to be maintained.

This new role, to which Orage gave himself completely, was an unforeseen source of the 'intentional suffering' Gurdjieff ascribed as one of the conditions of a more conscious state. Orage succeeded to some degree in interesting those who were studying with him to give money to the Fontainebleau fund, some by augmenting the group-meeting contribution which was nominally $2.50, always waived for those who could not afford it.

It was a surprise for Orage to find that most of the money collected from his groups came from those least able to contribute. Of course, there were liberal donors among the more affluent, but like rich people everywhere, they too had other obligations which for them took precedence. So Orage was driven to renew his campaign in all aspects, again and again.

There are members of the early groups who recall the penurious way Orage lived, his tiny apartment and office in an Armenian neighborhood. They remember also his worn overcoat and threadbare suits, which appeared not to matter in the least to him. He worked in every way he could: more groups, classes in writing, lectures on literature, writing of his own. He spared himself not at all and sent what he was able to earn or collect to the Prieuré.

Carol Robinson, who spent the entire summer of 1924 at the Prieuré, spoke to me of her astonishment at the steadfastness of the people, who cared for the kitchen garden, felled trees for fuel, kept the large house in order. They worked in pairs or larger groups, sharing their effort and, in their few spare moments, their understanding of the essential teaching. Carol and Jessie Dwight were on the Monks' Corridor, and not on the second floor where Gurdjieff's bedroom was, which the inhabitants of the Prieuré called the 'Ritz'. Carol reported that as she passed the Ritz on her way upstairs every night, two or three of the Russians were on their knees in front of Gurdjieff's door.

By late August, reports from the Prieuré were more optimistic about Gurdjieff's slow but steady recovery. Orage decided that he must go there to receive further instructions, and bring to the Institute a well-filled purse. Before leaving New York, he combined several groups into a large one, which met on lower Fifth Avenue in a studio belonging to Jane Heap. Gorham Munson agreed to work for the rest of the summer with the combined group, where they studied the ideas and sent a goodly sum to Fontainebleau.

In other ways as well, Orage was reassured by what he found at the Prieuré. Gurdjieff was definitely recovering. The pupils there were carrying on with the essential inner work, as well as the physical maintenance of the place. In spite of the difficulties, they had not allowed themselves to sink irremediably into passive discouragement.

No one seems to know the instructions Gurdjieff gave Orage in that short visit except that he was to return to New York, go on with this work there, and find ways and means to help support the Prieuré. Just as imperative for Orage was his concern for his flock in New York. He and they were trying together to understand and practise the Gurdjieff teaching until the hoped-for return of the teacher. This included maintaining the classes in the sacred dance, which had begun in New York under the supervision of Jessmin Howarth, an Englishwoman who had left her work as choreographer at the Paris Opera, first to learn and then to teach the Gurdjieff movements.

In the autumn of 1924, Orage had had little more than two years of study with Gurdjieff, and had counted on receiving more material, both for his own understanding and to pass on to his groups. But he was left to guide his pupils as well as he could from his own knowledge and experience.

Orage had never had difficulty attracting and inspiring people – as lecturer, editor and friend. But this situation presented a wholly new and troubling role: to interpret, with a minimum of distortion, what he was himself still learning, not with his head alone but with the whole of his being.

The idea of the difference between having 'information' about the work, which depends chiefly upon the head, and the 'knowledge of being', which includes all of one's perceptions, was difficult to convey. Judging from the time and effort it took to penetrate even a little into what Orage was saying, the idea of being, as well as its reality, seemed incomprehensible to most Westerners at that time. Many of the group members were, so to speak, conventionally unconventional, and thus more open than most to the question of ultimate meaning. None the less, the general education, molded under the influence of nineteenth century positivism – what Gurdjieff enjoyed calling 'their maleficent education' – had formed a shell around each person that was hard to crack. In general, the members had been brought up to admire scholarship as the highest human achievement, and could not for some time understand that a still higher aspiration would concern itself first with the level of a scholar's being. For them, intellectual levels were still what counted, which the modern world had long since substituted for levels of being.

It would be fair to say that what Orage was seeking, and why he sought out Gurdjieff in the first place, was the intensification of his own being. Confronted by the necessity of finding his own way to the direct practice of Gurdjieff's teaching, he allowed himself to speak to others only of what he himself had experienced and understood. He had to keep sharing the manna from Heaven, as it were, after it had ceased falling.

Many of those working with him were reading books written by Orage long before his meeting with Gurdjieff and were astonished to find much material in them that anticipated what was now given as part of the Gurdjieff ideas. Naturally, they asked Orage about it.

'True,' he said, 'I had found some of the ideas earlier. They were beads, and some of them pearls. But before I met Gurdjieff I had no string to hang them on. Gurdjieff gave me the string.'

6
The buried bone

Of any means of knowing if an intelligent God exists, our Science is completely indifferently ignorant.   A. R. ORAGE

In the summer of 1925, when Orage returned to the Prieuré for the second of his annual visits, Gurdjieff was on the way to full recovery. Lisa Delza, who was also there that summer, says that he was active in a quiet way. He would sit silently on the veranda, or somewhere in the great house, writing. From time to time, the people there would meet in the salon to hear de Hartmann playing the piano or listen to something Lisa then knew very little about, which was being read aloud in English.

Actually she was hearing the first awkward attempts at the translation, chapter by chapter, of the book Gurdjieff was working on, *Beelzebub's Tales to His Grandson*.[1] This was to be his major opus, which would embrace all essential knowledge. That it was actually in progress signaled the fact that work in quite a new form was beginning again in earnest.

Beelzebub's Tales aroused hope and also presented great difficulties for the pupils. From the first it was a most exciting, impenetrable and frustrating work to read, and, at that moment, to translate into English. This work, this *oeuvre*, which when finished was aptly called by P. L. Travers 'a great, lumbering flying cathedral of a book,'[2] was to contain, in symbolic and often in literal terms, the knowledge we were all hungering for.

Gurdjieff made a vital distinction between 'knowledge' and 'information'. For knowledge to be rightly transmitted, and properly received, a special effort was required to read and inwardly digest. Gurdjieff held that knowledge, like all else on this planet, was material, was food and had to be properly ingested and absorbed. And, since the way in which knowledge entered the psyche was of primary importance, it was necessary for him to write so that the very structure of the material would refuse to allow the reader easy possession of its substance. The translation must carry the same qualification.

Gurdjieff's statement that *Beelzebub's Tales* contained 'everything' was perhaps his reason for calling the series of books it began *All and Everything*, making a distinction that is so often missed between the sense of the whole and the infinitude of particles which make up the whole. The 'digging' that the reader must undertake to reach any understanding was essential. In fact, as Orage discovered, when an idea appeared to be too easily grasped, Gurdjieff's instructions to him were to bury the bone deeper.

The story the book undertakes to tell is of the education of a young boy, Hassein, by his grandfather, Beelzebub, who has long been atoning for the arrogance of his own youth, and who wishes his grandson to learn the process that leads to the acquirement of being.

Each chapter opens the questions of life and of human history so that Hassein, and the readers, can see the illusions that hold humanity in a state of near hypnosis, and be led to seek a knowledge of reality in order to break through the dream into a waking state.

As understanding grows in Hassein, the hope is that it will grow in the readers, leading them from mechanical, illusory hope to a knowledge and concern for the real possibilities life contains, and to an objective hope for humanity.

Orage's work, that summer and the next in Fontainebleau, was to translate into English the material that Gurdjieff had ready. First it had been translated from Gurdjieff's Russian to pidgin French, then into approximate English. Orage worked over the manuscript under the sharp eye and acute ear of Gurdjieff, whose unfailing recognition of the *mot juste* in a language he scarcely knew was uncanny. How he sensed that the word 'pianola' conveyed a nuance that 'piano' did not is an instance that comes to mind. Such sensitivity was a source of delighted appreciation to Orage.

What delighted him less were the Russian women who surrounded him at his work, interrupting him to tell him the words he must not use, even though they did not understand the connotations in English. It may have been their first attempt at translation into English from governess-taught French that made Orage say, on seeing their first draft, that the translation was hopeless.[3]

The account written by Thomas and Olga de Hartmann[4] of their preliminary work on *Beelzebub* makes clear enough what Orage was up against. According to them, Gurdjieff wrote or dictated to Mme de Hartmann for hours, and she spent many more hours typing and retyping his material in Russian, until she arrived at a text he approved.

The next step was Thomas de Hartmann's literal translation into 'English' (her quotation marks), then the pages were given to Orage to be put into 'real English'. But that was not all. Orage's translation was checked against the Russian text and he was asked to explain again and again why he used a specific word or phrase. One of Orage's best phrases, 'common presence', which is so much better than the French translation's 'présence générale' was typical of the sort of argument he had to win. (Many years later, a professional translator regarded that phrase as a stroke of genius.)

As each chapter was read to Gurdjieff, he seemed to rejoice at hearing his long and elaborate phrases translated into excellent, readable English. Orage sensed Gurdjieff's approval, though Gurdjieff sometimes asked another person at the Institute, whose literacy was certainly not equal to Orage's, what he thought of a word or phrase. Gurdjieff impeded egotistic satisfaction. Nobody was long in danger of flaunting a 'peacock feather'.

After two summers of such work, requiring patience as well as word-seeking, Orage returned to New York in the fall with a few translated chapters. The book soon became the center of gravity of the meetings. People would take turns reading it aloud, and then together ponder its meaning. Gradually Orage began giving his interpretation, basing it on the primary theme of the book, the attainment of understanding. And, he would add, understanding of a kind that required an altogether new mode of thought.

Beelzebub's Tales produced a powerful effect, but that is not to say it was readily grasped. There were layers of meaning that people were touched by, but could not in any way formulate. How should they regard this book? was the question. Could one listen, as Orage advised, without giving way to constant verbal associations and unrelated imagery?

Orage's effort was to unveil the material so that people would take literally what was meant to be literal and symbolically what was meant to be symbolic. Much of the narrative was addressed to different levels of perception in people (Gurdjieff had said seven). The task was to respond with the whole of one's mind, and not just with what Gurdjieff called the 'formatory apparatus', that part of the brain which was busy classifying ideas and objects, putting them into pigeon holes, and thereafter returning mechanically to them as statements of truth. This was all before the days of the computer, but his description of the conclusions of the formatory apparatus bears a close resemblance to computerized thought.

Delighted as he was at Gurdjieff's recovery, Orage found himself still in the same teaching role as more people came into the groups. Jean Toomer, who had witnessed the desolation at the Prieuré during Gurdjieff's illness, was encouraged by Orage to undertake groups of his own. A magnetic figure, well over 6 feet tall, Jean with light brown skin, sporting a trim mustache, looking for all the world like an emigré Brahman, is now best remembered as the author of *Cane* and canonized as a pioneer of the black literary renaissance. Gurdjieff had told Toomer that he ought to work with his own people, and many of them were attracted. But his groups soon included Americans of all kinds and in time he went on to Chicago, and still later, carried the work to Portage, Wisconsin.

Orage liked and trusted Jean, talked candidly with him, and wrote to him frankly of his difficulties with their common teacher.

Another pupil of Orage's who began to collect people to study the Gurdjieff ideas was Daly King. First Orage undertook a group in Orange, New Jersey, where Daly lived, and later persuaded him to lead one himself. For a long time, according to Daly, Orage visited his group regularly and consulted often with Daly. After the publication of *Beyond Behaviorism*, in which King 'sought to show the relation between scientific psychology and the ideas', he took a group in New York as well. Orage supervised the meetings at first and later took to dropping in from time to time. 'Of course,' King writes, 'he was always in the background. He was always *there*.'

In the summer of 1926, Orage went again to Fontainebleau to continue work on the translation. Several New York people were also there that summer, according to Lisa Delza. Daly King reports that he attempted to visit the Prieuré, rang the bell marked 'Sonnez fort', but was not admitted by the doorman. Orage was doubly furious: at the stupid doorman who failed to recognize a friend and at Daly for not insisting on entrance. Gorham Munson was more persistent and found his way in, in fact, soon took his place among the field workers. He stayed there humbly until the arrival of Orage, who told Gurdjieff of Gorham's work in collecting large sums of money for the Prieuré and sending it there with absolute regularity. Gurdjieff at once offered him tea.

When Orage returned to New York in the fall with new chapters of *Beelzebub* he had translated, he began reading again from the beginning with two purposes. He wanted to listen carefully, since he continued dissatisfied with his translation; his other concern was collecting more money for the institute. For though the Prieuré was beginning to take on the life that many visitors bring, more expenses had to be met than was possible with the money collected for summer rentals. His solution was to ask the members of the groups to pay $100 apiece to hear the whole book read. Lisa Delza, who remembers that moment well, adds that as always, those who could not afford that amount paid what they could or not at all.

That same year Orage ran into difficulties with Gurdjieff because of his continued interest in Jessie Dwight. Orage admired her independence of spirit, and Gurdjieff certainly noted it. Often while at work in the garden at the Prieuré, the workers in search of self-knowledge would stop for a cigarette or simply to rest. But when the figure of Gurdjieff loomed upon them, they would hurry guiltily back to work. Jessie, on the other hand, would go on serenely smoking her cigarette. On one such occasion, according to Jessie, he invited her to join him inside for one of his Turkish specials.

The next summer when Orage was in Fontainebleau, Jessie was not with him. Since they were now betrothed, Orage promised her that he would return on 1 September. And, of course, he told Gurdjieff the date of his prospective departure as soon as he arrived.

All that summer Gurdjieff busied himself and Orage with other things than the translation. He organized exciting motor trips with himself as driver – the best and worst driver in the world. In spite of many reminders from Orage, not all of them subtle, no move was made toward the translation. On the eve of Orage's departure, Gurdjieff announced that the next day the work on translation would begin. It could not have been easy, but Orage replied that he was leaving for New York the next day. What Gurdjieff said in response, I do not know, only that Orage felt rebuked. But he kept his promise to Jessie.

When we asked Orage about the event, he would reply that he understood Gurdjieff's attitude, and saw how the matter must look to him. 'He regarded me as someone who had, so to speak, come with him from another planet with a task to carry out. But I fell in love with a native, and this interfered with his aim.'

In terms of that metaphor, his fidelity to his promise was disobedience to his teacher. Orage's further explanation was disarmingly simple: 'I ran out of my first marriage. I will never do so again.' He cared deeply for Jessie, but his reason was more than personal. There was the double-headed question of two essential, but contradictory, inner calls. He used to quote from the Gnostic writings: 'Follow yourself and you will find me. Follow me, and you will lose both me and yourself.'

7
A passion for understanding

Do not tell me, as I have often said to biographers, what porridge had John Keats, or what earthly experiences befell Shelley. Only in so far as these things show in style are they of any possible value.

A. R. ORAGE

In the early spring of 1927, I was first taken to a 'Gurdjieff meeting'. The person who invited me, thus unwittingly changing the course of my life, was the Russian sculptor, Boris Lovet-Lorski, who admired Gurdjieff as choreographer. He had seen demonstrations of the Gurdjieff movements in Paris, and spoke glowingly of them.

The meeting was held in a large room of faded elegance in the Murray Hill section of Manhattan, belonging to Muriel Draper, a woman of much vitality and a salty wit, and architectural critic for the *New Yorker*. I found myself in a milieu that later became affectionately familiar.

There was a fireplace at the end of the room, giving out so little heat against the March night air that Boris and I kept our coats on. Some thirty-five or forty people were already seated in irregular rows of unmatched chairs. Everybody seemed relaxed and expectant, yet no small talk disturbed the unconstrained silence. Only a few were as young as I and, in general, all those present seemed to be what we used to think of as upper Bohemian – the men a bit tweedy, the women, to my fashion reporter's eyes, more individually stylish than fashionable.

In a few minutes a rangy, big-boned man who was not Gurdjieff entered the room. His name, my companion whispered, was Orage, pronounced like the French word for 'storm'. The newcomer settled his farmer-like frame into an armchair. His strong, bony hands, which looked as if they knew what they were about, extracted a cigarette from his side pocket and lighted it. As he looked searchingly at the people in the room, his large hazel eyes paused to take in the two strangers, as though asking us why we were there.

This was no effete public-school Englishman; more likely, I remember thinking, an Armada Irishman. (Later I learned that his mother's maiden name was Sarah Ann McQuire.) After a contained pause, in a deeply centered voice and in precisely articulated, non-Oxford English, he began to speak. I remember well the gist of what he said.

To continue our conversation on the subject of man's nature, man is in essence a passion for understanding the meaning and aim of existence. His work on the planet is to encounter, overcome and create obstacles. His aim is to fulfill the potentiality of his Being. As Gurdjieff says, he is born incomplete, and his task on Earth is to complete himself. That is the position of man on a cosmic scale.

But what is man as we see him on our own scale? How can we come to know who we are? What, as we see it in ourselves, is the state of man? What is my own state? Who am I? How can I know myself as a whole and in depth? What is my relationship to the world in which I live?

Seen by hindsight in the light of today's climate of inquiry into the human condition, how contemporary these questions sound!

The response was immediate and the spontaneity of the questions made me realize that these meetings must have been going on for years, as indeed they had been. I was unable to follow much of the discussion, though the others were quite at home, disagreeing with one another and freely admitting doubts. What struck me was Orage's attitude toward them: he welcomed their questions and actually seemed pleased when doubts were expressed. He decried credulity and actively supported true skepticism – which he defined as the acknowledgement that one does not *know* – as the road to truth. This was no self-styled guru making ponderous revelations. This was a man guided by reason, whose swift intellect seemed free of mere intellectuality. Much later I was to learn that he defined reason as the sum of all man's functions.

At a certain point, the clarity of Orage's thought and the simplicity of his language produced an expectant silence. He lit another cigarette, inhaled deeply, then, holding the cigarette between his fingers without taking another puff, went on with something entirely new to me: the exposition of the Gurdjieff ideas. He was not trying to convince or to impose a point of view. Instead, he was asking open participation in the examination of human life and its reason for being, beginning with our own. For my part, I found myself hearing what he said, not just associating verbally with his images.

That is not to say that I understood what lay behind his picture of mankind's state of hypnotic sleep and the mechanicalness of all human behavior. But what came through was principial in a new and inclusive way, not theoretical, not provoking debate, and altogether unlike talks I had heard and taken part in whenever the subject of the human condition arose. There was a pleasant informality about the meeting as Orage spoke through the blue haze of his cigarettes, and a sense of acute listening by all of us to the lucid flow of his ordered thought.

Strangely enough, the dire picture he drew of the helplessness of men and women, which meant all of us in the room, all the people I knew, all people everywhere, did not produce despair. Orage even went so far as to recommend experiencing despair as necessary for a genuine approach to the Gurdjieff work. The feeling he actually evoked, and which I felt all around me, was a wave of hope, which I was later to recognize as Gurdjieff's 'hope of consciousness'.

Not more than a week later Boris and I were invited to attend a small demonstration of the Gurdjieff movements, a non-verbal form of the Gurdjieff work, at the studio of the dance teacher, Rosetta O'Neil. This, Boris said, was what interested him most; there was something so authentic about them; when he saw them in Paris, he was very much excited by them, and their sculptural possibilities.

My own first impression was very different from his. What I saw were dancers going through ritual forms that did not

From an original lithograph of A. R. Orage by F. Ernest Jackson which appeared in *Neolith*, 1907

Gurdjieff in Hellerau in the 1920s

Gurdjieff when Orage first knew him, probably 1923

Orage in New York in 1930

entertain me, but produced wonder about what was going on in the inner life of the performers; they moved unsmilingly through difficult patterns that suggested a totally different kind of life from the one I was living. The movements were beautiful, I agreed with Boris, but puzzling.

After the demonstration we went with Hugh Ferriss, whose architectural drawings I admired enormously, and his painter wife, Dorothy, to their new apartment at the very top of a high building looming magnificently among its neighboring skyscrapers above chiaroscuro streets. The room was bare except for one armchair and a few unpacked wooden crates. The armchair was presented to Orage. The rest of us sat on the floor, except for one woman who looked around for a crate low enough to sit on, found it and sat triumphantly higher than the rest of us, where nobody could look down on her. At Orage's feet sat a handsome, blonde young woman. This I learned later was Jessie Dwight, who was married to Orage a few months later.

In answer to questions about how he had met Gurdjieff, Orage was soon telling us something about his own search, the way in which almost by accident he had come upon the Indian scriptures, which he spent years studying. Then, by accident again, he came in touch with Ouspensky and later, Gurdjieff. It seemed to me that he was saying that flickers of light touched us with no intention on our part, and I found myself asking him if he meant to imply that salvation could be a matter of accident.

'Well, why not?' he said. His answer shook me.

Later that evening I sat with him and Jessie, still in pursuit of an understanding of what he had said. I think now that he was questioning me in order to test whether I was suitable for the work, and the work right for me. In any event, that evening he told me exactly which group to attend, which books it would be helpful to read, and left me with the impression that I had been accepted as a member.

In the following months I found I had much in common with the members of this group. We shared a concern about the harrowing confusion of life, which was more than just personal, yet personal as well. All of us had our 'life' problems, which were not dismissed as irrelevant to the pursuit of higher understanding. Orage adjured us not to run away to some spiritual haven, but first to face our difficulties – with our bosses, our fellow employees, parents, husbands, wives, lovers. We were meant to look straight at our dreams and ambitions without inflating them and to search for the cause of the difficulty in ourselves. At the same time, only our best was permissible in fulfilling the requirements of our everyday lives. We were to learn to detach ourselves from agonizing over the troublesome psychological fragments in our inner kaleidoscope, and allow them to be shaken into fresher and more inclusive patterns. Orage helped us in a very practical way to unify these details into the question of the meaning of our lives, as we strove to see the whole picture, and to put every anguish, every 'fleabite' in its place.

Of course, when we first entered the group we regarded most of Orage's instructions as ideas. 'Your actual efforts are what count,' he would say. 'You need to experience, not just think about, the exercises given.'

What we were seeking was awareness without idenfication: a new state that we could reach only when we were truly awake. The taste was necessary if we aspired to live with disinterestedness, with a self-remembering that was the opposite of self-preoccupation. This could lead to another state of being, a word we pondered much and understood little. There existed a vital order in the mind, Orage told us, very different from its mechanical functioning. As his lucidity revealed to us the order he spoke of, we became somewhat clearer about what he meant by 'being'.

For myself, I began to realize how I had so often felt a gap in the intelligence of those considered to have superior minds, and why the judgment of intuition was dissatisfied with the conclusions of those minds. It threw light also on my reluctance to accept the dry interpretations of philosophy and scripture offered by some academics, who made me suffer by their cavalier treatment of the subtleties that required intelligent feeling for their full comprehension.

As the weeks and months went by, Orage increased the demand for inner work along the lines he had set out. Gradually we began to realize that in order to see ourselves with some degree of objectivity, we must try to observe as though the watched and the watcher were one. When the watcher became also the watched and 'action' took place, one felt oneself in movement and no longer tried to separate oneself from it. Orage called that state as we brought him questions about it 'participation'.

The next step was still far away for most of us. That he called 'experiment' to distinguish it from 'experience', and our effort in this regard was to undertake intentionally a specific kind of non-habitual behavior and carry it out with full awareness. In our work in movements, the structure of the exercise often gave us a strong taste of what was possible.

The Gurdjieff teaching, Orage often reminded us, had to be tried out in our lives and in our relations to those closest to us. He stressed the importance of loving one's parents and accepting to suffer remorse for the unseeing way one treated them. Every insight had to lead to increased responsibility for oneself and one's manifestations. There was nothing vague and distantly mystical about the search for increased consciousness, and before long I joined the others in gratitude to Orage for the light he brought to our concerns.

After a meeting, we would often troop off with Orage to a nearby all-night cafeteria. The dingy room, with the clatter of crockery and an unshaded light, became sun-dappled ground under a plane tree on the outskirts of Athens, where we sipped endless cups of watery coffee while the Socratic dialogue went passionately on.

Sometimes the talk deteriorated, as with our Greek predecessors, into hot argument among ourselves, which our modern Socrates did not interrupt but listened to with utmost attention. When appealed to for a solution, he would often answer with an electric impartiality, drawing effortlessly on his prodigious learning. It was, as A. E., the Irish poet said; 'Wherever I looked into Orage's mind I found the long corridors lit.' For us too, Orage was never imprisoned in narrow, fashionable cells of thought. In the end, he would bring us to an irresistible reconciliation, not compromise but a totally fresh way of seeing the problems that agitated us. We were breathing a new air and its plentitude was intoxicating.

After such a symposium our minds were sharpened with a fervor for understanding or, at least, pondering the questions that besieged us. What meaning, if any, was there in human life? What constituted true morality? How could we understand war? What is a man? A woman? Where was humanity's place in the universe?

It was usually late when we reluctantly moved towards home. Even knowing that in a few hours our jobs would be awaiting us, we would gladly have lingered in that dingy cafeteria the rest of the magnetic night. Several of us would take a taxi in common, dropping one another off along the way. Living the farthest downtown, I was often the last to leave the cab. I would mount the stairs to my room in Chelsea thinking how right Orage was in saying that a man could think only as deeply as he felt. What resolutions I formed not to let the charged impulse die out, to make more effective efforts to wake up, to be more aware of all that took place in myself, to be as removed from the petty as I had felt during the hours with Orage! I went to bed those nights feeling that eternity had penetrated the windows of my mind.

8
Sound and image

Before script, artists in words had also to be artists in life; and no degree in verbal finesse, I think, would have been able to persuade a seeing audience to believe its ears against all the rest of its senses.

A. R. ORAGE

The need to earn money for the support of the Gurdjieff work led Orage to undertake a series of lectures on literature, which evolved into a workshop for professional and amateur writers. It was a boon indeed for us Americans, still suffering in those days from uncertainty about our own literary capacity. How many gifted writers, like Hemingway, felt that they had to serve their apprenticeship in Europe!

The sessions were held on the second floor of an antique shop on East Fifty-third Street, belonging to Jean Herter, the son of a Brittany painter, himself knowledgeable in the fine arts, and his wife, Annette, a talented exponent of Dalcroze eurythmics.

As head of the workshop, Orage pointed out defects and shortcomings with pitiless precision. We braced ourselves to welcome this, and at the same time shrank from exposing our darlings to the healing light. Sometimes the fault was an insensitivity to rhythm, sometimes a question of taste, sometimes a writer's self-absorption and unawareness of the reader, sometimes error in structure, and so on.

Orage would read our prose aloud with what we felt was devastating mimicry. But often, when the victim was toppling on the last rung of despair, he would select a sentence or paragraph and, with a few deft changes, indicate how it could produce the desired effect.

Objective art, Orage would say, is art that achieves its object. And from the start he reminded us that writing was primarily communication, not what was then the fashionable term – self-expression. This may not have been a new idea, but he brought it to life. And the corollary of it was that a writer who had nothing to say would better be silent. He must feel, Orage said, 'a love amounting to a passion for conveying ideas – and love of the minds to which they are to be conveyed.'[1]

Without forgetting this high aspiration, Orage would return us cheerfully to the soil from which all writing draws its life: common speech. In the long centuries before literature was written down, the speaker had to seduce his listeners into paying attention:[2]

> Men had for thousands of years been content to be speakers and hearers. The demands on the artist in words in days before script were far more exacting than the demands made on the writer of today. He had to be able to capture, hold and direct the attention and sympathy of his listeners by the use of his personality, his presence and the range and power of his vocal and other resources. These demands, taken altogether, call for a Man.

We began to see that, even for amateurs like many of us, the purpose in writing was to bring forth in words and images the total intelligence of the speaker.

'In a thousand ways,' Orage said,

> the pen is hopelessly inadequate to convey the infinite subtleties of speech. Gesture, posture, tone of voice, facial expression and the movements Demosthenes called 'action' – these, together with the effect of the company of listeners, the setting and the occasion – how can they ever be conveyed in the record, however artfully edited, of the words only . . .? The despair that every writer must feel of ever producing the effect of speech, is anything but paralysing, except to vanity. Every writer to whom his art is religious – I mean, serious – has a goal and a motive, such as, as yet, no other art so clearly has. The plastic arts and dancing are *models* for life; but the art of the written word is an attempt to reproduce the life-model of perfected speech.

Well, we made our desperate little attempts to reproduce the life-models of perfected speech. Orage brought us down to earth in very practical ways. Could we decide who our readers were, and could we persuade them to read us? As professional writers, we should be at home in all literary forms. What is more, we should be able to communicate with people of all kinds and stations, temperaments and interests. Like Mark Twain, we should walk with kings and have the common touch. Some of us who had scorned popular journalism tried successfully to write for that market. Orage, joining in the exercise, produced a piece on the subject of money, which later appeared in *Fortune*.[3]

Whether we wished to enrich our lives with abundant variety, or to select and understand the best that the world of literature held, we knew that we were fortunate to be hearing Orage's illuminating talks on poetry and prose. His criteria were no mere intellectual classifications of literary material. We had to learn the art of listening, to become increasingly sensitive to sound and image, and even more so to the value of the idea involved. Only then, after this testing and after contemplation, could we judge where the idea belonged in the innate hierarchy of the mind.

When the workshop had gone on for more than a year, Orage suggested that we produce and publish an article or book on a subject we knew well. For Wordsworth's description of poetry as 'emotion recollected in tranquility', he insisted, was no less essential for prose. A spate of articles and books soon followed.

One of these was Muriel Draper's engaging memoir, *Music at Midnight*,[4] an account of her early life in the New England that no longer existed, except in the novels of Edith Wharton, and of her European years with her singer husband, Paul Draper, when their lavish entertainment required two adjoining houses on Holland Street in London. Here their friends came night after night to listen into the early hours to Thibaud, Casals, Rubinstein and Harold Bauer, playing for their friends with the ardor of youth. We all thought of Muriel, in whose drawing room we often met, as a born *maîtresse de salon*. She looked, as someone said, like one of the horses at the Acropolis, but to my eyes she was a Houyhnhnm of Jonathan Swift's, moving through the room with equine nobility. Though usually quite broke, she gave lively parties for artists, poets, musicians or just friends. Her memory was as amazing as her vitality, and each of the many persons that crowded into her house at any one time was remembered by name and foible. Her presence enlivened any gathering.

Another book that emerged from the New York vow came from Hugh Ferriss, architectural artist, whose drawings of New York were a haunting combination of prophecy and dream. *The Metropolis of Tomorrow*,[5] generously illustrated with Ferriss's drawings, suggested an ideal city on the island of Manhattan, washed by the tidal waters of three rivers and the sea. To leaf now through Hugh's shimmering vision of a city designed for human beings is to shudder once more at the reality of New York's Gadarene descent into real estate speculation.

Those already publishing were encouraged by Orage to continue. I remember such people as Samuel Hoffenstein, whose book, *Poems in Praise of Practically Nothing*, was a comic delight. Melville Cane was writing verse; Jean Toomer's work was appearing here and there; Mary Johnston, author of *To Have and To Hold*, whom I had read as a child, was trying new experiments. Isa Glenn was publishing *Transport*, which turned out to be her best novel. John Riordan, mathematician by profession, was publishing an *avant-garde* story collection. And the rest of us were selling articles and sketches.

Aside from the workshop meetings, nearly everyone saw Orage informally from time to time, bringing him some of the revised writing for more minute consideration. He was generous with his time and thought, and sometimes a lunch with him would determine the final form of the story or article.

One day, arriving early for a lunch appointment, I waited in the hall beside the telephone board, signalling the superintendant's plump and saucy daughter not to call him yet. Soon, from the elevator next to the bank of phones, emerged a handsome woman, emanating a bliss that lighted up her marble blue eyes, and so full of feeling was she that she passed us without a greeting. I recognized her as my favorite living poet, Elinor

Wylie, whose poem, 'Velvet Shoes', was my childhood's first walk in the snow, and whose *The Venetian Glass Nephew*, was my idea of the romantic novel *par excellence.*

Had she been seeing Orage? I wondered, and greeted him with that question. My guess was right, he told me as we walked the block to Arakel's, the Armenian restaurant in the neighborhood. We ate in silence the cinnamon-flavored rice wrapped in vine leaves, but when we reached the yoghurt soup, I asked whether Elinor Wylie was poetic in actual life.

'She is a true poet,' Orage said and added, 'She has known ecstasy.' There was a touch of reverence in his voice. After that I couldn't get another word out of him about her. He was an old hand at steering conversations away from personal questions.

Later in that same week, at dinner with Isa Glenn and her son, Bayard, I raised the subject of Mrs Wylie's visit to Orage. Isa was not reluctant to fill me in. In fact, it was she who had persuaded Elinor Wylie to see Orage. Mrs Wylie had been highly dissatisfied with her work, could learn nothing useful from the critics, and her friend of that time, William Rose Benét, himself a poet and critic, was unable to do more than reassure her. She had even kept from him her decision to see Orage, fearing his disapproval.

Mrs Wylie was skeptical of receiving help. Insisting that she felt something in her work was definitely awry, she begged Orage not to reassure her but to show her, if he could, what was wrong. She watched his face anxiously as he pointed out specific shortcomings.

As Isa recounted it, the problem was not mysterious. What Orage showed Elinor Wylie was that in both her poetry and prose she was using too many labials: the results were too rounded and lip-soft for the impact of meaning she wished. 'Substitute some gutturals where they are appropriate, and you will hear the difference.'

A few telling examples convinced her, and as they continued talking they sought out words with the throaty harshness or simple strength she wished to convey. Soon they left her personal concern with her own writing to speak of literature in general, and Mrs Wylie was struck by his knowledge and judgment. As she said later to Isa, she felt heard, understood and helped. Precisely what she needed had been given to her and she could now make use of it in the revision of her work in progress. In her words, Orage was a magician, and she was deeply grateful.

It is a rare gift – Orage had it – of rejoicing in the good fortunes of others. It is almost equally rare to rejoice in another's ease, to go to the great lengths of politeness and consideration to achieve it. It is the social form of *noblesse oblige*.

When Orage went on to enlarge another's attempt at literature, the donor forgot that his contribution was far from exact. By that time he was breathlessly and sympathetically following what Orage was saying as if he had (as indeed he had) played an important part in the development of the thought.

Ideas grew under Orage's nurturing like plants, and he never refused nourishment from fellow-gardeners. They all prepared the soil together, watered the plant, and let the sun shine on it. Then with joint delight, they watched it flower, become fruit and heedlessly drop seeds, which the gardeners picked up in handfuls and took home with them to discover later in their tidied-away thoughts.

Some of the workshop members had begun to meet at Christ Cella's basement restaurant in the East Forties so regularly on Wednesday noons that we called ourselves, with thanks to Christopher Morley, the Three-Hours-for-Lunch club. The cuisine was excellent but our real incentive was the chance to sit around a red-checked table cloth with Orage and, while breathing in fragrant promises from the kitchen, to talk with him. There was no lid on literary gossip, for instance, how Ezra Pound was getting along with his cantos.

But soon we would find ourselves launched on nobler topics such as the standard for literature inherent in the human mind, which could differentiate the temporary from the universal.

Often we would bring samples from what we had read, or written ourselves, and try to place them in the objective order demanded by their depth. If the samples were contemporary in tone, they were universal in substance, and we were astonished that we usually agreed on the place where they belonged. In his vast store of memory, Orage could always find something that fitted the distinctions we were trying to make, to discern the marriage of style and content. And with an easy transition, he would relate our findings to the order of cosmoses in the Gurdjieff system of worlds, showing us how to move from one scale to another. We were documenting the saying attributed to Hermes Trismegistus, in literature as well as in life: 'As above, so below.'

Orage maintained that the style was the man. To us it meant that if we read perceptively, we would penetrate a writer's gifts and weaknesses. It is interesting now to see how often he hit the nail on the head, for nowadays, when biographers spare nobody literary candor, we can verify Orage's opinion of a writer's abnormality, physical or psychological. One writer, who, from his style Orage diagnosed as syphilitic, is now known to have had the disease. Another who suffered from a diarrhea of words had the organic difficulty as well, and several whose rhythms gave away their homosexuality have since confessed, or boasted, of it. Orage's insight was never a judgment but an acute perception of illness through style. Study manifestation, he said, and you will know who another is – even who you yourself are.

Just about this time, a number of books by and about Katherine Mansfield were being published, some of them edited by her husband John Middleton Murry. We were enormously interested in that gifted, Chekhovian writer of short stories whom Virginia Woolf was later to confess she envied. Before that, she had endured years of increasingly debilitating tuberculosis, a disease not readily cured in those days. It had made writing difficult for her and disastrously interrupted her marriage.

Orage had known her well, indeed was the first to publish her stories. In one of her last letters to him, she says 'You taught me to write.' For a time before her marriage to Murry, their friendship became a love affair. Many years later, when Orage had been in New York, for several years, a curious visitor, G. C. Bowden by name, called at his office, saying that he wanted to meet Orage who had seriously affected his life. He turned out to be Katherine Mansfield's first husband, who told Orage that on a blustery day in February 1910, he had waited de the office of the *New Age* while Katherine went to inquire whether her first short story was acceptable. When Orage affirmed this, she went at once to her husband and told him that their marriage was over.

In 1921 Orage wrote an essay on her last conversations with him, 'Talks With Katherine Mansfield', which appeared in *Century* magazine that same year. (It was later published among Orage's *Selected Essays and Critical Writings*.[6])

She was no longer concerned primarily with writing as a craft, Orage says, but with the recognition that the mind, character and personality of the writer must acquire new depths. This was quite apart, she felt, from an improvement in technique, also necessary but more easily obtained.

After she had gone into detail about her new way of writing stories, Orage asked her if she really saw her way to it. 'I see the way,' she answered, 'but I still have to go it.'

'Only a few weeks later,' Orage says as he ends the essay, 'Katherine Mansfield was dead. I saw her a few hours before her death, and she was still radiant in her new attitude.'

Following her death on 9 January 1923, there was much gossip, favorable and unfavorable. It was some years before her husband, John Middleton Murry, said that Katherine had made of her time at the Prieuré, 'an instrument for that process of self-annihilation which is necessary to the spiritual rebirth, whereby we enter the Kingdom of Love. I am certain that she achieved her purpose, and that the Institute lent itself to it. More I dare not, and less I must not say.'

Ouspensky was simpler and characteristically direct:[7]

I remember one talk with Miss Katherine Mansfield who was living there [the Prieuré]. This was not more than three weeks before her death. I had given her G's [Gurdjieff's] address myself. She had been to two or three of my lectures and had then come to me to say that she was going to Paris . . . She already seemed to me to be halfway to death. And I thought she was fully aware of it. But with all this, one was struck by the striving in her to make the best use even of these last days, to find the truth whose presence she clearly felt but which she was unable to touch. . . . Soon after my return to London I heard of her death. G. was very good to her, he did not insist upon her going [leaving the Prieuré] although it was clear that she could not live. For this in the course of time he received the due amount of lies and slander.

Orage enjoyed informal gatherings and always brought something stimulating to them, sometimes a game. One spring evening he suggested that we choose quickly, intuitively if possible, the animal that best represented each of us. There was unanimity among us that Orage combined elephant and fox. A fox-like sharpness showed in the tilt of his nose, and he moved with the deliberateness of an elephant.

As traits of character, the animals we all agreed on for him were not far from the truth. His extraordinary memory was elephant-like and his shrewdness about people suggested the quick perception of the fox.

What also characterized him was a dry wit, as when he said that Bertrand Russell's felicitous style in expressing total pessimism sang like a doomed cricket on a dissolving iceberg. Or when he quoted with appreciation the dramatic critic, St John Ervine, as saying that Bernard Shaw's brains had gone to his head.

These days, whenever a few of us who knew Orage in those workshop days are together, sooner or later someone remarks that there should have been a Boswell among us to record Orage's conversation, an art form now lost.

Yet even a Boswell probably could not have conveyed either the gist or the full taste of the conversation we savored. For it was not only what Orage said, but the sureness with which he touched a person at the moment when the other was most sensitive and receptive. This was Orage's flair for evoking an inward impulse, an immediate search, which inspired the recipient to penetrate into unsuspected depths in himself.

Edwin Muir, poet, philosopher and critic, recalls this gift most vividly in his autobiography. 'Orage,' Muir says,[8]

was one of the most brilliant talkers I have ever listened to, particularly on the borderline where conversation meets discussion . . . His mind was peculiarly lucid and sinuous, and could flow around any object, touching it, defining it, laving it, and leaving it with a new clarity in the mind. From a few stammering words he could divine a thought you were struggling to express, and, as if his mind were an objective clarifying element, in a few minutes he could return it to you cleansed of its impurities and expressed in better words than you could have found yourself.

Muir writes from his knowledge of Orage in England. In America we felt this same ability, and I cannot help believing that conversation of his range and brilliance had rarely been heard before on this side of the Atlantic Ocean.

Muir goes on to say, 'This power was so uncanny that at first it disconcerted me, as if it were a new kind of thought-reading . . . He was a born collaborator, a born midwife of ideas, and consequently a born editor.'

This gift of Orage's was not thought-reading but probing for buried treasure, often unknown to its possessor. He felt and showed respect for another's mind, and selflessly encouraged another's insight. He did not cast a spell, as Muir implies; it was rather that his influence allayed the fear of seeming a fool in the presence of an expert, and allowed a truth, however modest, to find its way unhampered to expression.

Both in his literary work, and in his Gurdjieff groups, this same characteristic appeared. For often the most promising people, when sincerity was the criterion, were the least articulate, and so were surprised and gratified when Orage led them to their own formulations.

Orage's own writing was keen-witted, informative and often strikingly apt. His pared-down prose, his gift of epigram, gave rise to sentences that went to the heart of the matter with the skill of a literary sculptor. In the midst of the review of a book you might come across such a statement as, 'Religion without humanity is more dangerous than humanity without religion.' Both his talk and his writing had a way of touching any level of life without succumbing to the trivial. Events and ideas, even the most ephemeral or fashionable, were seen in relation to the whole that contained them.

Today, when Isaiah Berlin's brilliant essay, 'The Hedgehog and the Fox', is again being talked about, in which he divides writers and historians into pluralists or monists, I wonder where he, or justice, would place Orage.

When the essay first appeared many years ago, I, like other admirers of Berlin, was struck by the distinction he made between the fox, whose interests were diverse and many-sided, and the hedgehog, who believed that everything centered around one major idea or truth. The image comes from the fragment of a poem by the Greek poet, Archilocus, translated, 'The fox knows many things, but the hedgehog knows one big thing.'

Those who were natively hedgehogs include (according to Berlin) such world figures as Plato, Dante, Pascal, Dostoyevsky, and I would add Kierkegaard. The foxes are such believers in diversity as Aristotle, Goethe, Pushkin, Balzac and Joyce. In the essay, Tolstoi is placed as natively a fox, but one who wished mightily to become a hedgehog, who wanted the whole of life and its variety to be centered in a religious absolute.

Where does Orage belong according to this pattern? He wrote about, appreciated and took part joyfully in the diversity of life, offering his journal to all sorts of current concerns. Was he then a pluralist? Yet the scope of his knowledge and interest did not destroy for him the idea of the world as cosmos, not chaos, while the unending variety of life on many levels implied an inevitable order inherent in the human mind. Does this make him a monist? Through all this he remained essentially a questioner, even a skeptic. In his younger days, for example during his fascination for Nietzsche – he seemed a romantic. But even then, there were always classic overtones, such as his refusal to be seduced by the contemporary certainties of various forms of socialism. There also existed in his mind the 'medieval ghosts who speculate hither and thither in the hope of finding pasture for their souls.'

To epitomize my own impressions of Orage's character, I would say that he exemplified the trait he thought so essential to his own journal: brilliant common sense.

9
A classical romantic

Public opinion must pass through the purgatory of Atheism and Materialism before it is fit for Metaphysics without theology.

A. R. ORAGE

Was the Gurdjieff teaching becoming a religion for many of us avowed skeptics? Orage seemed to think so. He often reminded us that estoeric teaching, though at the root of all traditional religions, did not demand faith. It asked for inquiry, and finally transformation.

We searched the etymology of the word 'religion', accepting it as rooted in the Latin 'ligere', meaning to bind or to link, and recognized how bound or linked we felt to the major ideas of the work. When our behavior, or manifestation, was said to be the evidence of our understanding of the work, we raised the question of its relation to morality. For many people, Orage said, morality was a substitute for religious commitment.

His old journal the *New Age* published an article of his in the 22 April 1926 issue, in which he spoke of the role of religion in Gurdjieffian terms. He called it the 'neutralizing force that alone keeps the world on the middle way – when it is kept! – between the extremes of imbecility and madness.' He goes on to say that since 'the attempt to establish an ideal and conscious religion between man and man, without taking God into account, has failed, the only remaining hope of the serious social reformer is to "find religion", that is to say, "find God".' So much for Nietzsche's dictum that God was dead.

He follows this with an interesting modification of his statement to his secretary when he left the *New Age*:[1]

It would be saying too much to affirm that I resigned from

the *New Age* and from active participation in social reform in order to find God. I only wish that my motives would be as clearly conscious as that would imply. But at least I am clear now that no other end will end my search.

A perceptive friend of mine returned from France with Orage on the French liner, *De Grasse*. Since he was preparing a biographical sketch of Rémy de Gourmont, he was overjoyed at the chance of talking with Orage about his own literary venture. The conversations began, but soon the realization dawned that Orage's interest was not only in the beauty of a writer's style but in the substance of his thought. For ten days the two men read together and analysed chapters from a number of writers, English and French, and the biographer felt that he was given criteria he would never have arrived at otherwise. But, he added, Orage was not only deeply religious but primarily a moralist.

When I told this to Orage he astonished me by agreeing. Right discrimination in both the Buddhist and the Christian sense provided the criteria not only of what one thought and felt, but of how one manifested what one believed in life. Edwin Muir says of Orage:[2]

As a man he lived on the plane of antique virtue, and like Plutarch's heroes roused admiration not so much for his inborn genius as for the conduct of his life, his formulations and the control of his endowments. Consequently his life had a style, like his writing; a style achieved by a 'conscious' discipline which he concealed from the world, letting it speak for itself.

Will Dyson, artist and illustrator, says of Orage, 'Here was the secret standard by which we judged ourselves.'

In Orage's lifetime, much of our judgment of morality was limited to the realm of sexual behavior. I recall feeling rebuked at my own narrowness on reading Dorothy Sayers' remark that the church today was more concerned with the sin of adultery than with the far more serious sin of inhumanity of man towards man.

Often members of Orage's groups discussed the subject of a true morality, and what universal rather than provincial demands it would make upon us, which could reflect and nurture a maturing of the human mind.

Still in pursuit of that question, one evening after a meeting, Carl Zigrosser, curator of etchings, drawing, etc., at the Philadelphia Museum of Fine Arts, suggested we join Orage at a Childs Restaurant. Together we confronted him about 'objective' morality, sipping coffee until long after 3 a.m. Blond, handsome, Scandinavian Carl was having marital difficulties, which happily did not end in divorce, and was concerned about his personal application of cosmic principles.

In a mood that evening for the examination of his own past, Orage told us about his first marriage to a young woman who wanted to leave her family and thought marriage to him would achieve her independence. It cost him an Oxford education, because a certain Squire Coote, who thought highly of Orage and was willing to help him financially, disapproved of that early marriage. He was idealist enough to regard this gesture as the right decision.

Then a young revolutionary, when he returned home to attend his mother's funeral he wore a defiant red tie. Like his idealist contemporaries, he was taken with the notion of 'free love' which, after his marriage was over, led him into a love affair with Beatrice Hastings, who for some time was his chief assistant at the *New Age*. As he told us that evening, he met her on a London bus when he was returning from a lecture he had given at the Theosophical Society. She leaned over from the seat behind him on an open-top bus and, in an ardent voice, asked,

'Are you literary?'

'By way of,' he answered.

'I have written an epic,' she said. 'Will you read it and tell me what you think?'

Orage took the manuscript home and spent several astonished hours reading it, delighted with the author's skill and her mastery of poetic form. When she arrived at the *New Age* office to recover her poem, Orage invited her to write for the journal. Soon she was sharing his life in other ways as well, but much of the relationship seemed linked to her passion for the *New Age*, for which she wrote poetry, book reviews and articles.

At the moment when Bernard Shaw was implying that marriage was legalized prostitution and H. G. Wells, also a friend of Orage's, was living openly with Rebecca West, it was a natural arrangement for two idealistic bohemians to live together openly. And so Orage and Beatrice did, until she went on a long holiday to France with the painter Modigliani and began dancing nude on the tables of Paris cafés. What is left of that romance is a handsome portrait of Beatrice Hastings by Modigliani.

Orage grew thoughtful as he reminisced about his susceptibility to women, indeed his vulnerability. He spoke about his love affair with Katherine Mansfield as serious. He went so far as to say that he preferred her to Beatrice, but the latter, being more domineering and forceful had pushed Katherine aside. He now considered the episode a failure on his part.

With regard to women in general, he had many varieties of response. With some, he could sigh romantically that if only he were free, something he was never exact about could take place between them. Others he apparently pursued with offers and promises. In retrospect, it seems that he fluctuated between a kind of romantic flirtation that enjoyed the chivalric suffering of non-consummation, and boredom at being the target of unwanted attention.

Surrounding a popular and engaging figure there are always women available in many ways – platonic, maternal, conjugal, comforting, sensual – who offer themselves in various roles including that of lover. How guiltless is the object of all this? Orage's collaboration, as well as his nature, certainly helped to account for the deluge of letters that filled his mailbox, ranging from declarations of gratitude to astrological charts. Some of them, once he recognized the handwriting, he never bothered to read.

On one occasion, the rumor of a supposed love affair troubled him because there was danger of its reaching Jessie's ears. He asked me how such irresponsible gossip could have started? I pointed to his fireplace against the wall of his office, where I had just seen him toss an unread letter without putting a match to the pile collected there. The superintendent's daughter, who from time to time pushed a broom over the floor, could have been amply informed. 'I think that's right,' Orage said, amused.

But on levels deeper than his romanticism, in his life as well as in his mind, Orage remained essentially classical. Marriage, he felt, was a commitment that should be fulfilled as the vow it is supposed to represent. It created an atmosphere in which one could practise bringing about another's growth. And it was worth taking that desperate measure to learn what could be the love of head, heart and instinct. His famous essay 'On Love', which he modestly attributed to Tibetan sources, is an illuminating development of his own lifelong conviction.

Though not prudish about the love affairs taking place around him, he was, when his advice was asked, most specific. A married man among us who enjoyed adding to his list of conquests was, Orage told him candidly, taking an unfair advantage of marriageable girls. When the man insisted that his nature required him to seek monogamy from bed to bed, as Dorothy Parker wrote, Orage suggested that he select his victims from the less vulnerable, who could be participants and not prey.

In reply to a young woman's question about her suitors, as we still called them in those days, Orage wrote characteristically:

> I didn't need any evidence that you can always have them by the drove. The evidence I need is that you know them at sight and what to do with them. There are only three alternatives ever – alternatives, I mean, to a dead cut – a) friendliness, implying reciprocal service in the matter of food, and drink and jobs and talk; b) affairs – very, very occasional and most delightfully and whimsically conducted; and c) marriage. With this triangular meter, any girl, it seems to me, can explore the world of men.

10
Two rivers

The phase man is in, is for transforming impressions into a higher
order.   A. R. ORAGE

In the spring of 1928 Orage told us that Gurdjieff's work was
centering around his writing, now that his health was no longer
in doubt. With attention chiefly on that, he had none the less
decided to allow more people from America to spend their
summer vacation at the Prieuré, if they wished. As always,
Orage explained, money was needed to continue the work, and
those who went to Fontainebleau would pay for room and
board. It was not necessary, however, to live on the second
floor in the extravagant 'Ritz'; one could always take a modest
room on the Monks' Corridor.

Over the years, mixed accounts had reached us from those
who tried to enter the Prieuré. Some had no difficulty getting
past the gate; others said they had been turned away. Our
opinions were divided between the notion that sincerity was
being tested and the lack of judgment of the fallible gate-tenders.
It seemed, at any rate, to require a gift of persuasion to be
allowed entry.

Recently, however, group members returned from the
Prieuré with tales of hard, invigorating work in the gardens and
the kitchen, of feasts after what had seemed fasting, of Turkish
baths on Saturday evenings, and a general sense of beginning to
understand what was meant by 'harmonious being'.

None the less Gurdjieff seldom left his writing to supervise
the work, as he had done when the Prieuré was first opened.
People felt his presence and were always rewarded beyond

measure when he appeared at a meal or spoke individually with them. Most of the work was supervised by the older students.

Pleasant and unpleasant events took place in New York that same year. Orage and Jessie, who were married late in 1927, were now awaiting their first child. New groups of interested people were coming to hear Orage, and many were taking movements classes.

In addition to his task of providing money for the Institute, he now needed more for himself and his family. Some of his time and energy had to go into that. The writing workshop was again in action, and now evenings were begun, devoted to psychological exercises to test and develop quickness of perception and thought. Orage had discovered or invented them, probably a judicious mixture of both, and soon his friend and admirer, the publisher John Farrar, asked to publish them in book form, which Orage agreed to.[1] He wanted first to test them with numbers of people.

On the unpleasant side were minor rejections of Orage, which puzzled his friends as much as they appeared to leave him indifferent. Since Herbert Croly, editor-in-chief of the *New Republic*, admired Orage and the *New Age*, he asked him to analyse a current issue at a weekly staff meeting. With his unsparing critical sense, Orage unknowingly stepped on a few sensitive literary corns, Edmund Wilson's, for instance, for which he was not to be forgiven by the then Soviet-oriented members. As late as 1951, Malcolm Cowley, for many years on the staff of the *New Republic*, made inaccurate references to Gurdjieff, not even taking the trouble to spell Orage's name correctly.[2]

Also puzzling to Orage's friends was the refusal to admit him to membership in 'The Meeting Place', a club over Lee Chumley's restaurant on Bedford Street in Greenwich Village. In those speakeasy days, some of us who often dined there started a club for cultural purposes. One evening when Orage had dinner with us at Chumley's, the owner, Lee, came to our table. Charmed by Orage, Lee proposed him for the club. Years later the reason for the rejection filtered through: the communist fellow-travellers, of whom there were many in the club, felt that Orage had abandoned socialism, which was not really the case. We felt this was another instance of the prejudice of the near and far left against philosophical or spiritual inquiry.

Again in order to send money to the Institute, Orage wrote fifteen essays which appeared in a journal called *Practical Psychology*, edited by Gorham Munson. Long after Orage's death, they were published as a book, and have since been many times republished.[3]

We now aspired to understand the meaning of what Gurdjieff called the two rivers: the energies of our inner and our outer lives. How could we live in both of them at once, as Gurdjieff exhorted us to do? Our jobs, our everyday life demanded energy and attention, and the Gurdjieff work told us to do whatever we did as well as we could. We must be sensitive to, and participate in what was happening in the world and not succumb to spiritual pretensions. How indeed could we live in both streams at once?

As my notes of these days verify, my colleagues at the newspaper office felt an apprehension, as I did, that the world was approaching a climax of some sort. For those who thought that money could be made easily by the right manipulations on Wall Street, there was a get-rich-quick movement, and with it the sense that a destructive financial thunderstorm was pending. We felt the tension, waited for something to break it, and feared the break.

At the paper, there was much talk about the economic situation throughout the country. The financial section was invariably optimistic and explanatory, even when the first signs of high interest rates for loans and the closing down of small businesses appeared on the inside pages. Hoping time would prove him wrong, Orage was none the less convinced that some form of economic disaster was inevitable.

Friends went gaily off to Europe for the summer of 1929, quite sure that the profits made for them by their brokers would more than pay for the holiday.

This was still in the days before high income taxes. Costs were rising, but profits were outstripping them. For those who believed they could make fortunes by buying stock on margin, it was a summer of wild speculation. During this mounting intensity, Orage sometimes wondered aloud as he talked to us about where this hysteria might lead.

Having been invited to talk to groups of people living in California, Orage and Jessie drove across the country. As usual with Orage, he had an additional aim: he wanted to see what was now going on in the Theosophical Society to which he had once belonged, and he found some of his old friends there. The groups of people brought together by a distinguished elderly lady, Miss Bulkley, brought Orage many questions about the work he was now engaged in, and tried to prevail on him to stay for a while in the West.

Whatever else the journey gave him, he now had quite unexpected impressions of America: its beauty and vastness, the great topographical variety from the sculptural hills and valleys of Arizona to the gigantic redwood forests of California. Another strong impression was the friendliness of the people and the great possibility they suggested. When we asked him, after his return, about the spiritual character of the religions and cults already burgeoning in California, he gave his opinion that Jesus Christ was *not* a Californian.

The general optimism in New York boded well for me. The editor of the section that held my daily column suggested that I go to Paris to cover the fashion openings. My college instructor in philosophy, who was interested in my interest in Gurdjieff, was also going abroad and asked me to join her.

Orage gave me a letter to the Prieuré, admonishing me not to let us be turned away. We had no such trouble as Daly King recounts, though we pushed the bell tentatively enough. Who ushered us in, I do not now remember, as we walked toward that lovely old house, catching a glimpse of the formal garden.

Soon we were in the salon, where I first saw Gurdjieff. (Later we discussed the sudden sense of increased vitality we both felt.) Swarthy, stocky, mid-Eastern – he was all that I had expected. But I was not prepared for the look in the great black eyes, a light coming from a great depth, having in its stillness a movement that seemed inner and outer at once. There was also an extraordinary quickness in his glance, as if he had photographed us in full detail with the accuracy of a microscope.

As Americans introduced by Orage, we were given the red-carpet treatment. We were invited to remain in the salon and hear Mr de Hartmann work at the piano. In no judging mood, as we might have been at a concert, we listened fascinated to the unfamiliar Eastern sounds. G. sat silently with us, his very presence increasing our excitement.

Afterwards we were invited to share a frugal but tasty lunch, to which we gave our full attention since there seemed to be almost no conversation among the twenty or so men and women who looked genuinely foreign to me. The dining room was as quiet as a monastery. After lunch, one of the visiting Americans took us on a tour of the grounds and delighted us with the rumor that Gurdjieff was coming to New York within the next few months. My friend and I went back to Paris to job and duty, wondering how we could manage to spend next summer at the Prieuré.

When we returned to New York there was a sense of foreboding in the newspaper office. Many friends were still traveling in France, Italy or England when one lovely autumn day the stock market crashed. Whether one had much or little or nothing, we were all stunned.

While we were wondering if our jobs would last, from the adjoining office came the first personal shock: an editorial writer we all liked leaped to his death from a high window. Soon there were more such suicides. With all this drama came the realization that our assumed prosperity was over, and that we must now be more realistic and practical. We were not yet in want perhaps, but we began reading the future pessimistically.

The future of the work was in question. Would it be possible to continue to send money to the Prieuré? Would this economic crisis send Orage back to London, where we heard he was being asked for urgently?

One woman in the group who had always been well off complained before all of us of the descent in the value of her securities. Orage replied rather sharply that all she had lost was the gilt edge, and that many people were in real difficulty. Lightly, but penetratingly, he added that he was not at all sure that we could continue to afford him. Though he had foreseen the inevitability of the financial crisis, it looked as though the actual moment took him by surprise as it had the rest of us.

In our work with him, we were now studying the chapter of *Beelzebub* called 'Purgatory', which seemed most apropos. Our present, so involved with the subject of the past, present, and future, was taking on a new intensity. In answer to his grandson's questioning, Beelzebub told him that even His Endlessness, God Himself, had been threatened by the flow of time, the 'merciless Heropass', as Gurdjieff called it. Since time as succession, the linear aspect of time, was all that we generally experienced, it was also all that we knew from birth to death. Was anything possible in the period that was our lives?

Our effort, or perhaps more truly, our hope was to respond to the readings with the whole mind rather than with the formatory apparatus. The attention we searched for we hoped would include and blend all our perceptions.

The unfamiliar words peppering *Beelzebub* were meant to free us of our usual associations, we knew, but they also stood in the way. We found ourselves occupied with the etymological origins; were they Armenian, Arabic, Russian, Greek, or were they totally invented? Did it really help to call the Law of the Octave, a new idea in itself to most of us, 'Heptaparaparshinokh', which seemed a mixture of Greek and Turkish? No doubt it stopped us long enough to listen more carefully to its application in a sentence. It was certainly not a language for gossip at cocktail parties, as one of us remarked, and it made wiseacring (a favorite word of Gurdjieff's) impossible. But sometimes a word would reveal its meaning, such a 'being-partkdolg-duty', which clearly relates to the duty of a complete human being.

The book contained definitions and suggestions. Reading it aloud with care was the best way to get closer to its meaning. Most of us, however, did not then have access to the book unless we were asked to make ourselves useful by typing a chapter.

On the first occasion that I had this assignment, I felt like an initiate. Not being an expert typist, yet wishing to produce a perfect copy, I was up a good deal of the night on 'The Fruits of Former Civilizations and the Flowers of the Contemporary',[4] a censorious account of the culture of ancient Greece and later,

Rome, which we had always taken as the beginning of Western Culture. It was many years before I realized that Gurdjieff was attacking speculation for its own sake and the separation of the faculty of head logic from the other forms of human perception.

His use of the word 'contemporary', which was always pejorative and spanned more time than did our understanding of the word, is a clue to the source of his criticism. The Greeks were the first to move away from intuitional thought, and to develop a kind of rationalization that changed radically the manner of thinking of the whole Western world. When its influence entered Christianity in the Middle Ages, creative thinking gave way to dialectic, such as the now-ridiculed scholastic dispute about how many angels could stand on the point of a needle. Whenever Gurdjieff, in the character of Beelzebub, encounters defective thinking he calls it 'contemporary'.

We asked Orage many questions about the way to understand what Purgatory said on 'Time'. 'Duration is an aspect of time,' Orage said:

> We perceive only those phenomena that have some duration, but many periods of duration are too rapid for us to perceive the intervals between them. Duration of time varies for different percipients. We think it difficult to perceive the third dimension of time, though in a sense we are constantly perceiving it, because every being we meet is one of our potentialities. The universe we see is ourselves in the third dimension of time.
>
> Time is the sum of our potential experiences, the totality of our possible experiences. We live our experiences successively. Succession is the first dimension of time. To be able to live experiences *simultaneously* is adding a second dimension to time. To be aware of this simultaneity, is solid time, or the third dimension of time. When we have identified ourselves with time, as Revelation says, 'Time shall be no longer.'
>
> We struggle with time in order to extract experience. The more aware we are, the better use we make of time. We think it is our enemy because it will not wait for us to have our

experiences. The flow of time through us gives us our chance to extract what we can.

Then Orage summed it up in an image:

Time is a three-fold stream passing through our three centers (mind, emotions, instinct). We fish in that stream. What we catch is ours. What we don't catch is gone. Time does not wait for us to catch everything in that stream. If we catch enough, we have enough to create the three bodies and become enduring.

But our relation to time had to be immediate. Our work is to live, be aware, in the present. As Rabbi Hillel put it centuries ago, 'If not now, when? If not here, where?'

When he talked with us informally as well as in groups, Orage seemed to us to be in both streams at once: the inner and the outer. His deep concern was for the state of the Western world, which was becoming so chaotic economically that a spiritual search would soon be regarded as a luxury.

For more than six years he had been meeting the demands of the Gurdjieff work with his most passionate attention. But now, he wondered where he could serve best the vital needs making themselves felt. Was it time for him to test himself again, to put his energies and talents – journalism and public speaking – to work in the old forms but in a new way? From hints he dropped from time to time, there is no doubt that he was reconsidering his role – in the work and in the world.

11
A simple man

Every kind of being – invertebrate, vertebrate, man – has its own field of impression. With the field appointed for man, every man has his own status. Each man is said to have a garden in the whole field given to man. His status in the cosmic scale depends on the tilling of his own garden. The point of view we are asked to cultivate is that of a cosmic engineer.   A. R. ORAGE

In the fall of 1929, Orage verified the rumor that Gurdjieff was coming to New York within a few months. Now we were to have an opportunity to put questions to the master, and there was time to prepare ourselves for it as well as we could.

Orage gave us no idea of the form our encounter with Gurdjieff would take, only that it was certain to be wholly unexpected. Our preparation must intensify so that in Gurdjieff's presence we would remember our essential aim.

There were, of course, practical preparations to be made, and we were soon hastening to find the ·right quarters for him, agreeable but simple because he did not like anything '*bon ton*'. In the end, we settled on the Great Northern Hotel on Fifty-seventh Street, not far from his beloved Carnegie Hall.

All this entailed more collections of money. What sums would be needed to cross many palms with silver so that Gurdjieff would not be held up on his arrival? There was enormous interest in foreseeing everything we could, a sort of competition to please him and gain his approval. As his arrival approached, anticipation rose, and by Christmas time hope pulsated in all our gatherings.

As soon as we were sure of the hour the ship was due to land, Orage commissioned two of us, Dorothy Wolfe and myself, to go to the pier to meet him. I was astonished to learn that Orage was not planning to go. 'Be sure to ride back with him,' he instructed us.

Many welcomers were already at the dock when we got there,

stamping their feet and blowing on their hands against the cold of a brilliantly sunny, freezing winter day. While waiting for Gurdjieff's party to appear on the gangplank, I began to review my first impressions of Gurdjieff last summer for the short time I actually saw him, and reflected on my failure at reaching the disinterested level of attention that I had hoped for.

An uproar on the dock under the letter 'G' cut me abruptly from my meditations. At the center of it, dressed in a conventional dark blue overcoat, which a caracul collar to match his astrakhan fez, was Gurdjieff, his great dark eyes glowing. In a pleading tone, he insisted on keeping the twenty-five melons he had brought with him. The officials gesticulated their inability to admit the melons on grounds, as I gathered, of botany, biology, immunology, entomology, etc. Quite naturally to government officials, melons were a Trojan horse for the secret entry into the country of hostile insects.

'They special from Persia,' Gurdjieff declared, in a more authoritative tone. I watched and listened to this first example of Gurdjieff's well-known way of manipulating rules and the people whose duty it is to uphold them. In the end he won the day and the melons. When I was invited to partake of them some time later, I was vastly disappointed at not finding in them some rare exotic flavor testifying to their far-off source in an ancient land.

With all this distraction, I did not forget my instructions to ride back in the taxi with him. Helped by my friend, Dorothy, I slipped in beside her in the cab, pushing past an unknown member of Gurdjieff's 'tail', as he liked to call his retinue, who took the seat in front with the driver.

Once on the way, puzzling over the difference between the present impact of the man and my imagination about him, I took the chance and asked whether he would allow a question.

'Tell, tell,' he said.

'Would you be kind enough to explain to me what you mean in *Beelzebub* when you say that time is the unique subjective?'

He looked at me, smiled, and said in a tone so appealing that all my brashness vanished, 'Truth, I very tired now.' It was a full minute before I saw that I had been deflected in my first attempt to steal wisdom from the tree of opportunity.

Gurdjieff's lithe movements on the dock had put me in mind of a great cat – a lion or a puma – with coiled strength, which he could unfold at will. Indeed, as I recall what I felt in the Gurdjieff that I saw then, the dominant impression was one of force. To my eager gaze, he was all Being; a natural phenomenon, a mountain stream of energy which could flood in a torrent or bide its time as noiselessly as water in a well.

These memories bring to mind now the difference between that figure of overwhelming power that stepped off the boat on a day so long ago and the still powerful but no longer stormy patriarch of his later years, whose chief characteristic was compassion. In the twenties and thirties those great dark eyes, gleaming with intentions we could hardly guess, could make us shiver at a glance. The black staghorn mustache turned up at the corners, the whiplike quickness in pointing out a man's chief fault, perhaps in one devastating syllable, did indeed cause many to fear him.

Both Gurdjieff and his teaching have been decried by some as lacking in love, that many-splendored word. It is not surprising that the timid were put off by his candor, his perspicacity and, most of all, by what we used to call his 'look'. For some it was a loving, impartial statement, but there were others who dreaded it. All of us, whether we loved or feared him, or took turns doing both, recognized Gurdjieff as formidable.

On his last visit to New York in 1948, some fourteen years after Orage's death, the black mustache had faded into a soft white, and the outer fierceness to open kindness. Those who met him then for the first time could not believe that he was ever considered as lacking in love. In a recent conversation with Jessie Orage, as we sat warming ourselves before the fire in her fifteenth-century cottage, we both spoke of the impression of compassion Gurdjieff gave on his last visit.

'That's the real Gurdjieff,' Jessie said emphatically. 'All the rest was a role.'

In truth, Gurdjieff mistrusted our fatuous use of the word,

our exaggerated idea of our capacity to love anyone but ourselves. For him love was a state to be achieved.

'Practise with small animals,' he used to say. 'They are simple
for you.' He went further and suggested that we practise with
flowers. Those who read his face, as he watched people wasting
the opportunity of their living time, understood that this prophet
was weeping for the sins of Jerusalem.

In the chapter of *Beelzebub's Tales to his Grandson* called
'The Terror of the Situation', there is an account of the work of
a 'messenger from His Endlessness', a saintly personage named
Ashiata Shiemash. In Persian and Arabic, I am told, this name
can be translated as 'a ray of the sun'. On a marble tablet, which
Ashiata Shiemash left behind him, were detailed the action of
the three 'sacred being-impulses' of faith, hope and love. With
regard to the last the tablet says:

> Love of consciousness evokes the same in response.
> Love of feeling evokes the opposite.
> Love of body depends on type and polarity.

To that last sentence was added in an earlier version of *Beelzebub,* 'and lasts as long as the substances of which it is composed.'

To return to that unforgettable moment in 1929, the taxi took
us from the dock to the Great Northern, a good but by no
means smart hotel. A second taxi with others who had met
Gurdjieff was behind us. He stepped out of our car, strode past
the entrance and moved eastward, looking around as though
expecting someone. I at once thought that he was looking for
Orage, but there was no sign of him. We followed Gurdjieff
single file – though I would be at a loss to explain why – really
looking this time like a tail, and when he made a complete turn
back to the hotel, we moved in a snakelike curve behind him.
At the door, he turned and invited us upstairs.

In a sitting room fitted out perfectly for a traveling salesman,
he looked incongruous, like a caged tiger, though one who had
chosen his own cage. We sat wordlessly with him until he broke
the silence by saying that he was thirsty, not for 'alcool', but
for a simple drink. Something was ordered and soon a glass of

Orage in New York in 1931

Orage in New York in 1931

Gurdjieff in New York in 1934, after the death of Orage. Gurdjieff was in New York when the news arrived

Gurdjieff in Paris in the last year of his life, 1949

tonic water was handed to Gurdjieff. He rejected it. It was too flat. On being given a second drink, this time ginger ale, he pronounced it too sweet, fit only to spoil children's stomachs.

I watched all this, uncomfortable because the right drink had not been found. 'Why don't you mix the two?', I suggested. Gurdjieff looked at me with interest.

'Make! Make!', he said. So I took one bottle of ginger ale and one of soda water, combined a portion of each in a glass, tasted the mixture and presented it to him. He sipped it thoughtfully, as he might have sipped wine, nodded his head and spoke with a seriousness that made me feel I was about to receive an honorable award or – more valuable still – an impression that he thought I needed.

'Intelligent,' he said, 'you use head in right way.'

In recalling my feeling of that moment, I have thought since of what Gurdjieff often said about his writing: everything should be taken in seven aspects. The overtones of that down-to-earth remark about a practical matter set a sudden review of my life, with all its superficial thinking on which I had long prided myself, unrolling before my inner eye. The vision reached its painful climax with our ride in the taxi and my pretentious question. To me it was that bit of verbal acrobatics, with no grounding in my own life, that had seemed intelligent.

This was my first experience with the way in which Gurdjieff's presence could produce an inner revolution. It usually began with feeling myself lost in a whirlpool of confusion, then sinking very deep toward absolute stillness, and finally returning with the taste of a limitation I had refused to see. There I go, imagining that I could understand the nature of time from another's explanation, when I could not truly understand my question. Could I, as a matter of fact, understand anything without first knowing how to meet what the moment required? Then a true question might be born of hunger, not intellectual curiosity. Yes, Gurdjieff had put me where I belonged. Yet strangely enough, he had left me with a lively hope of finding a way to move toward the truth of things.

Long before the hour set for the meeting at Muriel Draper's, most of us were there, expectantly awaiting the appearance of Gurdjieff and Orage.

As the men walked in together, the contrast in their gait was striking: here was the Middle East and there was the West. Gurdjieff moved effortlessly forward, exuding force, looking as though the business suit he wore was a masquerade. Taller and heavier in his tweed jacket, Orage was differently alert, the whole of him intent, and his hazel eyes shining like a fox.

Two chairs were in front of the room and, as Gurdjieff seated himself in one, Orage pushed the other slightly behind. We were all watching every movement. Many of us had never seen Gurdjieff before and stared at him with a fixed attention, like cats at a mousehole. Here was our teacher and our teacher's teacher.

Then, in a sudden shift in role, Gurdjieff began playing the country cousin. He plucked at the lapel of Orage's jacket and said shyly, 'Orage, you take charge.'

'This is your group, Mr Gurdjieff,' Orage said.

'Orage, Orage,' he replied, 'you explain better. I very simple man.'

So it was going to be theater. In the gravest of voices and with the timing of a music-hall straight man, Orage intoned, 'Mr Gurdjieff wants you to understand that he is a very simple man.'

The room filled with bursts of laughter, none heartier than Gurdjieff's own. It was refreshing that being serious did not require being solemn. And when we were all relaxed and responsive – though I don't believe we were ever entirely free of strain in his presence – Gurdjieff began to unfold his plan.

Meetings would be set up to serve two aims: to give material to people in groups and to earn money for the work. This second aim he spoke of, with a kind of jovial mockery, as 'shearing sheep', though for the most part he referred to Americans as burros, rather than sheep. The French emerged somewhere in the talk as 'donkeys', while the Russians became 'turkeys', a cross between the peacock and the crow. Offensive as these terms may sound, the atmosphere in the room was such that no one was offended.

The theme was frankly the need for money. As always, burdened as he felt with the perennial task of collecting money for the work, Orage made it clear that those who could not pay could serve in other ways. From among the men, Gurdjieff appointed 'gods', who were to be in charge of admission to meetings, collections and keeping the meeting-place in order.

Readings from *Beelzebub's Tales to His Grandson,* in Orage's latest translations, were to be given in two series: one, on Monday and Wednesday evenings, would cost $5 a week; the other, on Tuesday and Thursday evenings, would cost $25. Fridays were reserved for a special activity: Thomas de Hartmann would play the Gurdjieff music for us. There would be no charge.

For those who wanted to study *Beelzebub* more intensively, there would be opportunities in the daytimes. They could have individual consultations with Gurdjieff at specified hours. Also, after checking with the gods, we might invite outsiders to both the lectures and the music.

Thus began the evenings which turned out to be educational in more than one sense. One of my first discoveries – after I had cunningly put myself down for both the reading sessions – was that there was no difference between the $5 and the $25 evenings. The same material was read in both.

Determined to get my money's worth, I tried to give my best attention to Beelzebub's instructions to Hassein and, through Hassein, to us. I succeeded in listening more carefully. That is not to say that my understanding was at all clear.

There is no doubt that many of the others in our old groups were also experiencing concern and reassessment during this period, when we were no longer meeting in the old way. We saw Orage informally as often as we could, hoping to get closer to what was taking place and what it foreshadowed.

Orage came to most of the studio meetings, sat in the audience attending carefully to the reading, obviously concerned for the accuracy of the translation and the best way of putting the ideas as expressed in the book into comprehensible English. Sometimes both men were together after a meeting, presumably discussing the chapter just read. Afterwards, we often went with Gurdjieff to have coffee and Orage was not always with us. After such an occasion, we would talk to one another tentatively about the fear of losing Orage and the fact of our dependence on him.

12
Limitation and expansion

More radiant than the sun, purer than the snow, subtler than the ether
is the Self, the Spirit within my heart. I am that Self. That Self am I.[1]

Dazzled as we were by the presence of Gurdjieff, most of us
turned to Orage again and again to understand a comment or an
instruction. Our naive Western way required direct, unequivocal
explanation of this mythological moment. We needed some way
of knowing how to breathe in the atmosphere that surrounded
Gurdjieff.

We watched as he sat in catlike relaxation on his couch, one
leg tucked under him, stroking his mustache and looking from
one to another of us. He had the air of being in two worlds at
once, as Orage put it, and in his presence, one could not imagine
wishing to be anywhere else.

These tastes of freedom made us realize how seldom we were
out of the prison of suggestibility and habit. Around him, our
usual sufferings were, as Gurdjieff put it with his customary
imagery, fleabites. We began to glimpse how trifling were our
angers and anxieties in the face of a major shared problem: the
human condition.

Yet all this came about with such simplicity, for Gurdjieff
used direct language in his contact with first-, second- and
third-degree pupils. When someone's face showed astonishment
at what was just then happening to him, Gurdjieff enjoyed
picturing a calf who, after frolicking in the fields all day, returned home in the evening to confront his familiar barn door,
which had been painted another color. I don't know if a calf's
jaw drops, but ours could.

Orage helped us to assimilate powerful impressions and see

better the scope of Gurdjieff's direct teaching, how his observation ranged from the most minute manifestation to a perspective that included the universe. Something rare was almost within reach, we felt, but perhaps at a high price. Orage agreed, adding that we might find it impossible to pay that price. But something was up to us; we must insist upon receiving what we needed, and not just accept being shorn like sheep. It was difficult, if not impossible, to carry out Orage's advice. No price seemed too high for the happy vitality that allowed us to bear the discomfort of sitting long hours on the floor in a crowded, stuffy room, pushed and prodded by others. But we aspired to go beyond that to a state of attention which, for me at least, had hitherto been impossible.

Orage reminded us that we were in the presence of Being – hitherto an abstract word to most of us. We made efforts to describe our impressions. For me, it was not unlike being in the presence of a great natural phenomenon. At the Grand Canyon, for instance, I knew I would not be able to remember what I was seeing, and lacked the ability to take it in even while gazing down into it.

Since those days I have had the good fortune to be in the presence of great teachers in the fields of psychiatry, Vedanta, Buddhism, Samkya, Islam, Tibetan Yoga, and whatever category Zen will allow. Each of them was unique: Carl Gustav Jung, Daisetz Suzuki, Jiddu Krishnamurti, Sri Anirvan, Karmapa, – and others who like them exemplify great and universal being. What good would it do to compare them, since each has his own special quality? But to give words to the specificity of Gurdjieff: he was a spiritual giant in whose presence we felt the limitation of our own personal world.

To return to that moment, Gurdjieff evoked in us both wonder at what could be and a recognition of what was. The very feeling of expansion, strangely enough, brought with it a realization of our limitation. Certainly I did not feel pumped up with the kind of illusion that fades on the morrow. It was rather that I was infiltrated with an energy I hungered for but did not know how to keep.

The relation with Gurdjieff was also of a new kind for me. In some ways, he was like a grandfather: I felt an intimacy as with someone I had known for a long time, who understood, accepted, and valued me as I was. On the other hand, he could withdraw to a great distance, leaving me feeling banished.

One evening, with Orage's approval, I invited to the *Beelzebub* readings a young man who, though skeptical of metaphysical concerns, was curious to see the indescribable figure of Gurdjieff. At first, I was sharply apprehensive about his reaction, but as soon as the reading began this anxiety vanished.

There were some hundred or so people in the room, but we had found a corner where we could listen comfortably. Whether my concern about my guest had made me more sensitive or whether the quality of attention in the room was aiding me, I was listening as never before to what *Beelzebub* was saying and able to hear the message. When the reading ended, I found that my breathing had grown very quiet, as if it also had taken part in the listening.

Gurdjieff, standing at the door as we made our way out past the 'gods', gave me an inquiring look. I introduced the young man and explained, 'He is hearing *Beelzebub* tonight for the first time.' Gurdjieff nodded to me and, without glancing at my companion, said, '*You* hear it tonight for first time.' I was startled that he had seen what was happening in me, for he had seemed to pay me no regard during the evening. And I began to realize how much is visible to one who can see.

This was my first experience of Gurdjieff's lightning perception of another's inner event. From then on it was evident that almost never did he fail to see, and in some way remark, the onset of a change in state in another. He might even murmur 'Bravo!' when for a moment someone woke up to the real world, though there had been no sign that the rest of us could distinguish.

Much activity was going on both in Gurdjieff's apartment and in the one above his, where the de Hartmanns lived. Preliminary translation of *Beelzebub* in preparation for Orage's editing was taking place; some people were writing, some were reading the already translated texts to study more intensively what they had heard. Mme de Hartmann was in charge, allocating the material as Gurdjieff had specified and receiving money from those who contributed it for the privilege of studying the texts.

Often Gurdjieff would meet people privately at what he called his office, which consisted of a table in Child's restaurant at Columbus Circle, not far from the apartment he was now in. Orage was often by his side. Many came, waiting at nearby tables until he was ready to see them, to the delight of the management and the extravagantly tipped waiters. In Paris, Gurdjieff's office was the Café de la Paix, where those waiting for him dallied, not with the famous Child's pancakes, but with café Liègeois.

In the evening Gurdjieff would invite a number of people to his apartment for supper, which he often prepared himself. He was a superb cook, with a knowledge of exotic herbs and spices that transformed freshly killed lamb and ordinary eggplant into *haute cuisine*. One of the appetizers he often had was a salad containing all the usual ingredients – greens, tomatoes, red peppers, sweet basil, tarragon – into which he had tumbled bottles of chutney and a species of dill pickle obtainable only in a special delicatessen in the Bronx.

When sometimes an Eastern delicacy was brought to him, he would divide it into enough portions to share with the others. For those of us who took part in these prolonged feasts, there was never much sleep, but then very little was needed with the largesse of energy we received. Indeed many of us learned that second wind was followed by third wind, and sometimes even by a fourth.

At Gurdjieff's request, Orage arranged a weekend evening at Gurdjieff's apartment for a group of literary people, including several publishers, to hear a reading from *Beelzebub*. As an admirer of Orage, John Farrar, who was about to publish his *Psychological Exercises*,[2] helped him with the selection of guests.

Among ourselves, we discussed anxiously which chapter we thought should be chosen, and agreed almost unanimously that the one to avoid, if we wished ever to see the book published, was the newly-translated chapter on 'America'. It was not just because of the ironic treatment of the American psyche and its various manifestations, that made us reluctant to have it read to strangers. The truth was that we ourselves felt let down by it. It seemed to us to have nothing new to say, to be without any effluence of sublimity and, in a word, banal.

Besides, we were concerned, as Gurdjieff himself never was, about the impression he would make on sophisticated outsiders. Orage alone remained serene and I could not tell how much he shared our forebodings as to which of the diverse Gurdjieffs the visitors would see, how he would act toward them, and whether he was really serious about publishing that porcupine of a book at this time.

After everybody had been served a drink – a required courtesy in Prohibition days – the cocktail party conversation erupted. When Gurdjieff entered the room, the guests grew silent and looked expectantly toward him. His first act was to offend a woman whose decolletage he thought extreme, using words that American men at that time reserved for the locker room. Startled, the woman looked at her neighbors, some of whom seemed about to join her in an indignant exit. But by then, Gurdjieff was passing around Eastern sweets, Turkish delight, lychee nuts, halvah and the like, which were already being sampled by many who had not heard the remark, and in the general confusion the moment went by.

Gurdjieff then signalled the reader to begin. Soon the social postures took on an air of dutiful but weary listening. For the reading consisted, as we had dreaded, of the chapter we wanted least to hear, 'America'. The guests grew restless, the chapter seeming to them boringly interminable, and to us painfully so. Finally one by one they began to slink away without expressing the usual thanks for a lovely party. The publishers looked embarrassed and one of them took Orage aside to tell him confidentially that there was no market for the book in its present stage. Perhaps the later chapters would make it more publishable; it was still too early to tell. Thus ended the first exposure to the modern world of *Beelzebub's Tales to His Grandson*. In retrospect, I cannot believe that Gurdjieff had any intention of publishing it. At that time he may well have wished merely to give Orage and the American groups some evidence of the hurdles such a book would have to surmount.

Still, in some quarters there was a keen interest in Gurdjieff, the man, and in his work, and a number of people tried to get in touch with him during that visit. Rom Landau, not a follower of Gurdjieff, says, 'It was not merely emotional men and women and certain types of semi-intellectual men who came under the spell of Gurdjieff. Men and women with pronounced critical faculties and a marked intelligence became his pupils.'

Landau's own curiosity about the man led him to write asking for an interview. He was then at work on his book, *God Is My Adventure*, in which he included an account of his meeting with Gurdjieff. Whether or not Orage had informed Gurdjieff in advance that Rom Landau was a journalist, a member of a profession Gurdjieff detested, he recognized Landau's type at once and was far from cordial. Landau did his honorable best to make contact, but the only patent result was a succession of physical reactions, which he ascribed to some magic spell Gurdjieff had cast upon him.[3] When I first read Landau's account I had just returned from a minor operation performed with local anaesthesia. I at once recognized the symptoms he described. They were exactly my own, before and during the operation: just being scared is what they were.

In any gathering Gurdjieff always set the feeling tone, and the farewell meeting before his return to France was warm and affectionate. Orage had explained to us that sheep had been sheared and thanks could now be offered to people carrying on the work in other cities as well as New York. There were also presents Gurdjieff would distribute: money to be given to children who merited a special education, and acknowledgments, often in the form of Turkish delight or halvah, to the Americans who had been so generously helpful.

Among the welcoming gifts to Gurdjieff from members of Orage groups when he first arrived was an excellent harmonium, upon which he could play the music he knew and compose the themes for new pieces. It was handsome, rather like a small, reddish mahogany piano. Rich sounds emanated from it, which did not blur, as our piano sometimes did, in the bass notes.

After telling us that we might come to the Prieuré as long as it continued, but that he could not now say what his plans were for the immediate future, he pointed to the harmonium and said he was making a special gift of it to Mr Schwarzenbach who, with his wife, had been the donor.

Some day, Gurdjieff declared, after he was gone, the world would take note of this event. The harmonium would by then have become a – there he searched for a word in English to convey the precise nature of the gift. He turned toward one of his pupils, named Metz, who hastily supplied a word: 'Souvenir,' he said. 'It would be a souvenir.' Gurdjieff was not satisfied and turned to Orage who was shaking his head. Gurdjieff asked him what *he* would say. 'Sacred relic,' Orage answered with an appropriate intonation.

That exuberant laugh of Gurdjieff's, sounding like a giant child's delight, rang out as it had many times during his visit. In light moments, the talk between these two men has been compared to the comic dialogues of Gallagher and Shean, footlight favorites of the period. It was as though neither Gurdjieff nor Orage ever forgot his part.

13
Something missing

Essence is the truth before God. Personality is the truth before men.   A. R. ORAGE

After Gurdjieff's departure in the spring of 1930 the tempo of our lives slowed down. We began to review more quietly what had taken place, and to ask ourselves and Orage what we now understood together. For though we could not wholly rely on the memories of our experiences, we knew that something had changed in us.

Orage helped us to see that something considerably more demanding is required than the mere realization of our petty shortcomings: our whole attitude toward ourselves would have to be tempered in the crucible. The idea of change, or transformation, called for unimaginably more than reforming this or that trait. We had been helped to widen our perspective from concern with personal achievements to a feeling of fellowship in the human race.

Psychotherapy and other remedies were not what we needed, but the candid view of the human condition, of which we were all a part: our pervasive sleep and its overwhelming evidence in the way we move and speak and go about our troubled lives.

Whether we could carry it out or not, we saw that we had to undertake a struggle with habit. And as explorers, we had to follow a course up the river of personality towards the still unknown reality at its source.

The Gurdjieffian glare had given us moments of seeing how mechanical even our precious emotions were. Our minds – if not our hearts – now knew how difficult it was to look even momentarily into ourselves, to say nothing of sustaining the insight; we knew better now what Gurdjieff meant when he said that this self-knowledge was 'no cheap thing'. Perhaps not much better, but a little better. From his height on Mt Meru, he had warned us that only inner work would allow us, in the end, to die an honorable death. And this meant learning to live an honorable life.

Though Orage usually spoke directly and without metaphor, we were now closer to knowing who the Tibetan evil spirits were and where some of the medieval devils dwelt – in our own psyche – even if we called them by the less fearsome name of negative emotions. We had come a tiny bit closer to the realization of how much we were held in thrall by unrecognized fears, and how general was the self-deception about this slavery.

We must face our ordinary lives less haphazardly, Orage said, and with more intention. It would be of little use to us if all that was left of Gurdjieff's visit was the memory of challenging readings, conferences, succulent dinners and shocks of awakening.

On his part, he was increasing his schedule of work. New groups were begun. In addition, subsidiary groups for intensive work were set up. The one I took part in was run by Daly King, under Orage's supervision. And again, there was the perennial need for money, which led Orage to take some writing groups quite outside the Gurdjieff work.

All this increased activity brought problems to most of us, who worked for a living. Some had jobs, which like my own, were quite demanding, so that often clever manoeuvering was necessary to fit 'work' projects into our weekly schedules. But most of us were young and vigorous, and we were presumably learning how to gather and make good use of the energy we needed.

Free evenings there were none, certainly not for Orage. Monday night we were at the main group, Tuesday with beginners, Wednesday at movements, Thursday at the writing workshop, Friday, the psychological exercises and, for some of us, Saturday with the small special group. I cannot remember now whether Sunday was actually free. Some Sundays we spent on pleasurable outings at the country house of Mrs Blanche Grant, but part of that day went into examining her notes and giving our version of what Orage had said at the last meeting.

From notes taken then, I have the impression that Orage was trying to sum up, as well as clarify, the ideas of the Gurdjieff teaching. Its essence, he made clear, was ancient and traditional. One by one he put the ideas into language that related them to the perennial spiritual teaching at the heart of the great religious and metaphysical traditions. At the same time, he threw light for us on the ingeniously modern and scientific-sounding terminology that Gurdjieff had invented to make these venerable concepts accessible to Western mentality.

'The bridge in ancient religions,' Orage said,

> meant the Way – the way of the Buddha, the way of Jesus. 'I' am the way, meaning not one's ordinary self, but what is really meant by 'I'.
>
> In addition to our intellectual, emotional and physical centers, there is a fourth center called 'I'. But never do we or will we receive an impression passively there, because the only impressions accessible to this center are taken actively. Not God and all His angels can *put* an impression there. Only 'I' can. Someone has to direct our attention to the existence of Fourth Center – with us, it is Mr Gurdjieff – but only 'I' can fill it.

He quoted the saying, 'The Mountains look on Marathon; Marathon looks on the sea.' The sea represents the outside world; and my usual self, my organism, is the Marathon that can look at that world, the sea. But only my true 'I', (the mountains) is able to look at Marathon, which is to say that only 'I' can see the whole of myself.

Since 'I' as the essential self was still a concept for most of us, even for those who had had glimpses of its inner reality, Orage tried to make clear the need to evaluate it properly. Usually we did not – our association with the word or the sound 'I' was not transcendental. We habitually said 'I' as though we had the right to do so. But sometimes we sense that 'I am' means that 'I' have a body.

'Jesus', he said, 'referred to the body as a temple. It is not our idea of a present-day temple, but one where drama, the arts, dancing, writing, and so forth, were carried on – something for all parts of the body to participate in.'

Orage responded to our repeated efforts to understand better the idea of essence and personality, and to discriminate between them in our observations. We felt the dual need to understand the cosmic significance of the idea, which required our thought to extend to quite another scale, and the practical effort to live with the whole of oneself, which called upon an intelligence we felt we lacked.

Orage's way of making us feel the scale of the problem, without discouraging individual attempts, inspired us to keep trying. We had his support, yet felt his own questioning, his own need for help. He was not Gurdjieff who *knew*, but a human being like the rest of us, though much more sustained in his efforts. But like us, he reached out for the substance his intelligence needed, and he did *know*, in himself, something that could not be shaken.

His talk with us on 'Essence and Personality', helped us to recognize the distance we were from self-knowledge and the need to put in question all we knew.

'Essence is God's truth about oneself,' he began in one of our Monday meetings,

in contrast to social and expected truth about oneself. Essence is irrespective of time, place and anybody else's feelings, – what one would dare to avow, if there were no consequences, of the statement of truth. Essence is the truth before God, as Personality is the truth before men: the contrast between the eternal state of being and the temporary, conditioned state of being: the difference between a soul in itself and a soul conditioned by the time in which it lives.

For us there was little time left. Soon we were to separate for the summer, and we felt a growing intensity in the main group. Orage urged us to make a deeper effort in our inner work, one that would lead to direct experience, and to understand better the major ideas of the Gurdjieff teaching.

He often referred again to the beads, the ideas that he had pursued many years before his meeting with Gurdjieff. Only when Gurdjieff had given him the string to hang them on, had he begun to understand the relation of the great human insights to the essential truth about man.

'Man', he would say, 'has a passion to understand the meaning and aim of existence.' But the passion had to be one's own, and we had to learn to 'work' as Gurdjieff had told us, to strengthen our wish. Orage reminded us that Gurdjieff had said he could bring us the conditions for work, but we had to do the work ourselves. We had to suffer through the many layers of misunderstanding, discard everything we found false. But did we really know how to work in this way? What was now required of us?

Orage saw that we needed ideas to sustain our efforts, even the recognition that we were not so alone in this dark world, that throughout the history of mankind, from time to time, what Gurdjieff called 'messengers from His Endlessness' had appeared to instruct, and give hope to, humanity. Those of us who had wandered away from the religious or moral teachings of our childhood, now returned to reexamine Christianity or Judaism, and found that we were better able to understand the Gospels and the Torah.

Orage responded to our realization of our kinship with the traditional religious teachings, and soon we were reading together the Buddhist 'Setting up of Mindfulness', the Dhammapada, the Upanishads, as we tried to ponder them. Books on Zen were just beginning to appear in English, and we read them, feeling that they were close relatives.

But where were the living examples of the level of being we sought? They were few indeed, we concluded. This must be what Gurdjieff meant when he said we did not have the 'ableness' to be Christian, that our first step was to become able to sustain an effort towards being.

Our response to Orage's stimulating review was our own pursuit of new and ancient theories, ideas and myths. We brought back what we found, anxious to share our latest discoveries with him, but it was clear that the 'knowing', with unshakeable inner certainty was not yet ours. He even complained that we challenged him too little, and we realized that we failed to make enough demand on him to compel his magnificent reason to search to the very limit of his capacity. Tranquil and dignified as he appeared, we heard beneath his criticism a cry for help. Something he needed was missing. After years of red-hot efforts of attention, what discipline did he now require? Where was the substance he needed?

On the one hand, he emphasized the need to make more intense efforts to understand and to practise the Gurdjieff teaching. On the other, something new was taking place in the relationship between Gurdjieff and Orage, which with hindsight we saw had already begun to take place while Gurdjieff was with us. We had all accepted as natural and right that Gurdjieff would take over the direction of the work while he was here, and Orage's attitude toward him during that entire time was impeccable. Our teacher's teacher had appeared to delight in Orage's seriousness and in his wit. But something had begun to change.

When we questioned him openly, as Orage had always allowed us to do, he would say unequivocally that Gurdjieff was his superior officer and that he was pledged to carry out his orders, that is to say, the exposition of his teaching, and those orders he obeyed.

So long as he remained with Gurdjieff, he would honor his pledge. He told us once more that Gurdjieff had given him the string on which to hang the beads of the essential ideas. Gurdjieff had given him priceless instruction, which brought him to insights he would never otherwise have had. But he had withheld something he had promised, some material Orage needed and wanted desperately. It was as though he knew that time was running out for him, and wanted to absorb whatever was still possible.

Sometimes Orage would speak of the way in which a great teacher, such as Gurdjieff, makes his disciples independent. He does not reason with them that the time has come for them to test their own understanding far from his immediate influence, but rather makes it impossible for them to remain near him. (We speculated whether this is what had happened to de Hartmann, Ouspensky, and others we knew or heard of.) In the end, after taking in and testing what knowledge one was given, it was necessary to trust what was reliable in oneself. On the one hand, obedience to a teacher for a time was essential. On the other, it had to lead to obedience to one's own higher nature. What, we asked one another, was Gurdjieff trying to teach Orage and the rest of us?

In his personal life, Orage seemed more fulfilled. By now his marriage to Jessie had resulted in his first child, a boy named Richard. For Orage, well into his fifties, it was close to a miracle to have his own child at last. Aside from his joy, and his gratitude to Jessie, he felt stability of a new kind. In a letter he wrote on 28 May 1929, he said:

> The baby, you will be sorry to hear, is developing out of all proportion to its nose, which is relatively out of joint. You must see it to believe it. Jessie is well, but I guess she'll have something to say on the subject of bringing up a baby that is not the same colour as her opinion on the subject of bearing one. Oh, one *does* learn by living!

For Orage, it was a living he had until then lacked. When asked by some of us how he regarded having a child so late in his life, he answered with jocular solemnity that Pythagoras had also waited until he had achieved something in himself before having children. But apart from philosophical explanations, Orage clearly rejoiced at this latest gift. Since his view was that we have no 'right' to anything in life, he could only be thankful.

It was many years now that we had taken for granted the presence of Orage, with his readiness to encourage renewed effort and his patient listening to our problems and difficulties. Touched to the heart as we were with unerasable impressions, we felt eternally related to him. But the flow of time was inescapable – the merciless Heropass, as Gurdjieff called it – and would bring inevitable change.

14
Farewell address

The seed is the ultimate object of the tree; all other elements are subservient to the seed. The seed when ripe is independent of the tree. In the same way man can become independent.   A. R. ORAGE

Orage wanted no 'broken hearts' when he met with us on 13 May 1930, to summarize our time together since his arrival in 1924. He said again, as he had so often done before, that the most fortunate event in his life was the meeting with Gurdjieff, to whom we all owed much. The Gurdjieff teaching, as he was to repeat in a letter he sent for all of us to see, was for him the very latest word of truth. If he returned, as he hoped, in January, there would be a new kind of work. It was in truth his farewell address.

'We are still far from that order of Being,' he began,

that can do without meeting or a director. There is a difference between a group and a circle: the latter meet for themselves individually, to help each other and to help a common cause, 'to make the world safe for consciousness.' Very few of us have a sense of these three responsibilities even after six years. Some have a sense of one. The first sense of individual responsibility is that unless I spend my day advantageously from the point of view of consciousness and development, I am lapsing, or disloyal. This is consciousness of the first side of the triangle.

The second responsibility is toward our neighbors, the members of our tribe also striving for consciousness. When you can say that no wave of circumstance is so high that you are submerged and lose sight of the method, you have developed consciousness of the second center. This is the first crystallization of individuality. And still I hear people complain that in a crisis, it is 'trifling' to talk of the method at such a time!

The third form of consciousness requisite for membership in a circle has to do with the work, in which respect I think we are weakest. Jesus' personality, as I have sometimes said, was not different from ours. He was not an occultist – not a Californian. He spoke of Living Jerusalem as the City of God – the circle of workers. His passion for Jerusalem was divinely paternal or parental. Theosophical literature speaks of the masters as 'the elder brothers of the race' – an ideal of a being who could not but be as an elder brother. You have heard of the patriarch and the matriarch; dissociate them from social associations and consider the quality which in a group distinguishes some as 'elders'. When it is really present, it indicates a state of being and a third center of gravity.

When a being has all three of these kinds of consciousness, he can be either a circumference or a center in a circle. Such members of a circle have a communion which is not perceptible but which is not occult either – it rises from their common understanding, their ability to be in each other's places. It becomes unnecessary for them to meet. You will realize how far it is necessary for us to go before we reach this state.

I will be back in January, for four months, but the same kind of work cannot be repeated on my return. So the terms of attendance at the group from January to April will be utterly different from those that have prevailed so far. I shall have to be independent of the group financially – no one will have to pay anything again to attend a group of mine. I shall have to see certain signs of development, of work done, in those who will attend the group. I shall know these signs even if you don't, and I shall know them however you phrase them.

There is an experience which comes when you know that you are losing your body and your life. Beelzebub, in the chapter on Gornahoor Harharkh's machine, thought he was going to be lost. Though such an experience lasts only a few seconds, no experience thereafter will be more than a trifle.

You will have known the fact of death. This is the kind of evidence I shall require for membership in a group.

No vow of secrecy will be required because you will not conceivably be able to repeat what you hear at the group. I have a conviction that if one of us has a problem that might impede the development of a group into a circle, it can be discussed objectively. Except in the absence of 'other self trust' one could not give away the facts of such discussions. But can we ever trust the majority of us not to misunderstand, or not to betray confidences?

A group must be selected which can be trusted to discuss problems as if we were dead and holding a post mortem. Also it is necessary that this group should make a greater impression on the community. In six years the impression we have made is almost entirely bad, associated with cult-like beliefs. We are more like Californians than like Akhaldans.

The kind of works that must be undertaken by a working group here are the establishment of a school like the Pythagorean, only not under a roof; an organization without organization. Take some subject in which you are relatively expert and start a group – if you are developing, there will percolate into the group something of this magnetic influence. Not everybody can undertake such groups, but teaching must be done – teaching of the ideas – and it must be done in connection with the technique in which individuals are skilled. If such groups were formed, they could be independent, like planets in relation to a sun which is the source of inspiration. I suggest that this work become obligatory in the New Year, with the threat that, unless in eight months you are a candidate for such work, you will either be compelled to attend a beginner's group or no group at all.

I aim to be absolutely independent of the group for my own needs, and the needs of the institute, and in this position I shall be able to speak candidly and to expect candid replies to those beginning circle meetings. Seriousness and determination will be of course the first requisite for candidacy. I am too tender-hearted to force the pace as Gurdjieff and Ouspensky can so ruthlessly do. But unless you are serious, I cannot be serious – you can hold me back.

I want to remind you once more of certain principles which you understand – to your peril, as St Paul said to those who were hearers and not doers; for if they had not heard, their not doing would have been without sin. Having heard, you incur the responsibility of doing.

The end and aim of the method is to attain the state of being in which your planetary body and all its possibilities become yours to exploit. The psyche comes into possession of a planetary body and by the law of reciprocal feeding, planetary food is eaten and transformed until it participates in higher states of being. Our feeding upon nature is a transformation into higher substances. And when I feed upon Orage, through self-observation, participation and experimentation, Orage does not suffer but comes up a step. I divinize my planetary body by feeding upon it. Self-creation by reciprocal feeding between psyche and planetary body is the end of the method. This attainment of the ability to exploit the planetary body is a common as well as an individual responsibility of all three-centered beings. There is cosmic development corresponding to that of the individual three-centered microcosm.

Here enter the ideas of objective morality which can, in my opinion, be set against any ethical code in existence, and from which no one can subtract anything or add anything. These laws make necessary many acts the omission of which society or convention do not condemn. No one's example can ever be followed.

The five points of objective morality are like the five fingers of a hand for handling situations. Number one means keeping the three brains of the body serviceable. Number two is constantly to be pondering the meaning and aim of existence – not necessarily with any hope of solution. Man exists to be the mind of God and as mind ultimately to understand the meaning and aim of existence. Preoccupation with this problem makes all other problems relatively easy. Once I defined art in life, for an artist, as the pursuit of ever unattainable perfection. Perhaps even for His Endlessness there is a secret He does not understand, in the pursuit of which understanding, the words of this method are tossed off like shavings.

Number three is the obligation to make Being-effort: the effort of doing. This is not necessarily a visible activity, or concrete work, but it is effort. Obligation of this kind is to keep oneself exercising – effort-making. Perhaps before January I can make for you a scale of exercises of will, from the scale of the mouse to the elephant. These would not be exercises of mind but of developing will, which is the ability to carry out 'whims'. I have received a suggestion from Gurdjieff which makes this possible.

Number four is to cooperate with others who aim at the same objective reason.

Number five is duty – to ease the burden of His Endlessness. Unless you make effort, it must be made for you. Now the burden is just upon His Endlessness.

The individual enters by self-observation into the order of being-responsibility and develops in this order of being according to these five laws of objective morality.

It is not obligatory for everyone to understand all the tenets of this work – cosmic chemistry, tables of foods, and so on; these are for specialists. But the practical aspects are obligatory for all.

Now having perhaps unfortunately listened to this, you are capable of sin – of the refusal to convert verbal form into formal understanding.

The following day Orage wrote to Stanley Nott, who was still in England. 'We had a farewell group meeting last evening and it would have done your heart good to witness the scene. I *love* the group; and I couldn't bear the thought of being long out of touch with them.'

15
An end of patience

Take hold tightly. Let go lightly.   A. R. ORAGE

Orage had been back in England for hardly a month when Allan
Brown received a letter from him dated 11 June 1930, giving us
the first clue with regard to Orage's conversations with Gurdjieff
about the future of the work:

> Apart from settling into our new abode and reviving my
> delight in English country, I've done practically nothing but
> ponder the question of my relations with G. Without having
> as yet come to any crystallised conclusion, I can say that my
> strong disposition is not to come to the Prieuré at all this
> summer. There appears to be nothing new doing there and,
> as for the translation, I'm fed up, as you know, with it, so
> much so that I refuse to work on it again *until* G. has finally
> precipitated the Russian text or is seriously preparing to pub-
> lish the English text.
>   . . . I told Gurdjieff in New York that I'd come to the end
> of my patience and that, without a new initiation, I was as
> good as dead about the Prieuré; furthermore, that I proposed
> to try the effect of 'growing chungaree' by myself – his reply
> was so unsatisfying that I shall carry out my plan. In other
> words, I shall stay here in England doing my best to get a
> new understanding of the Book on my own resources, – in
> despair, frankly, of Gurdjieff doing anything more for me
> than he has done for Stjernwall, Hartman, etc., however
> faithfully they have given up all to follow him.

Orage's reference to 'growing chungaree' refers to a sympathetic character in *Beelzebub* named Hamolinadir, a learned Babylonian alive during the building of the Tower of Babel. His inability, after years of research, to arrive at objective truth led him to give up his philosophic pursuit. 'Hamolinadir,' Gurdjieff says, 'was never again occupied with "sciences" and spent his existence in planting "choongary" [alternative spelling], which in contemporary language is called maize.'[1] So, like Cincinnatus of Rome, who, having had enough of politics, returned to his farm, and Voltaire's Candide, whose author, living frustrated during the Age of Enlightenment, returned to *cultiver son jardin*, Orage was also tempted.

In the same paragraph of his letter to Allan Brown, Orage adds: 'One thing remains unshakeably true, – the ideas are all the world to me, and I shall always be ready to cooperate in their spread provided I myself continue to increase in their understanding. What I cannot do any longer is to continue teaching without also learning, – and Gurdjieff has ceased to teach *me*.'

What were Orage's intentions? we asked one another. Did he mean to live in England from now on? What was the new life he referred to, that he would now undertake? What were his plans? His hopes? All we knew was that he and his family were spending the summer in Sussex, and we waited eagerly for any news.

Stanley Nott, who with his wife, Rosemary, had found a cottage for the Orages, reported that Orage was happy to be once again in English countryside. He found Orage wiping tears from his eyes as Rosemary played the Gurdjieff music, but not from sadness, he said. Mairet, on seeing him again, found him 'unexpectedly large and almost as surprisingly youthful as on my first sight some eleven years before, but there was a greater strength and dignity about him, a heightened self-consciousness and self-command.'[2]

Those of us left in New York that summer felt a sense of disconnection in whatever direction we looked. In what we were now calling our 'ordinary' life, we were less happily secure than we had been before the financial crash a year ago. No longer were we shocked every day with devastating changes: now they seemed inevitable. Among my friends in the Orage groups, a number had lost their jobs. Those who were lucky enough to have savings, began to live on them. Those well enough off were more careful about what they spent and were anxious about their future. That wonderful carelessness of Americans about the almighty dollar was gone. Among the unworried rich, the fashion was to pretend to be as poor as the rest of us.

If Orage was considering a return to journalism, from many points of view this was a good moment. The prophecies made by the advocates of Social Credit, of whom Orage had been the most eloquent, were beginning to prove true. Was he going to test himself again in his professional life, and follow his impulse of service to humanity, at the same time?

These were speculations on the part of his American friends, always ending in the major query of his relation to the work and to its primary teacher, Gurdjieff. In spite of Orage's letter to Brown, which some of us had read, we found it difficult to believe that he would cut himself, and perhaps many of us, off from Gurdjieff. Besides, he had promised to return to us in January, and we all knew Orage as a man of his word.

Actually Gurdjieff arrived before him, coming to New York in November 1930, and once more living near the Columbus-Circle Child's, where he kept 'office hours' and saw people as he had done before. He also began meetings again with the oldest group. Almost at once people began to question him about his dissatisfaction with Orage.

On one occasion I head Gurdjieff say that Orage had failed in his presentation of the teaching. He had placed too much emphasis on self-observation, which was only the first stage of the work, and had allowed too much wiseacring about the ideas. Gurdjieff's language was not always easy to understand, and I think he continued by saying that since we had been led astray by Orage, many of us were now 'candidates for lunatic asylum'.

There was a discussion by the more knowledgeable ones that I could not follow, but what filtered through to me was that many of those present accepted like sheep this derogation of Orage's work. Their attitude became so unbearable that I blurted out to Gurdjieff, 'If Orage made a mistake or did not know how to go on, it was your fault. He taught us what he learned from you, and you did not give him the additional material he needed.' I was appalled at my impertinence. For a long moment I waited to be slain.

'Bravo!' Gurdjieff said, looking pleased, even approving. At once my understanding of the whole event had to be revised. There was something in Gurdjieff's absence of annoyance that made me wonder what his underlying, *teaching* reason was for what seemed to us an attack on Orage. Gurdjieff was never petty. What was he trying to tell us? What did he want us to learn? What attitude was necessary to the continuation of the work?

One way to produce a new moment of self-recognition was the impact of a psychological shock. Were we by now too identified with Orage? We loved him, there was no doubt, but how much of that love was dependence and attachment? Certainly for such spiritual fledglings as we were, the love without identification that Gurdjieff spoke of, the 'love of consciousness' could easily have become an attachment to its human object.

But why did Gurdjieff smile with pleasure at my reaction, which was clearly 'identification'? Always, I recalled, he seemed pleased at an 'essence' response, something not learned and studied, but truly what one felt. Again the vision of Gurdjieff as a great, natural phenomenon was strongly present to me. But also present was the knowledge of Orage's years of devotion and unaided effort to share his deepest understanding with us. As I have tried since to compare my impressions with those of other members of the group who were there, I should say the consensus is that Gurdjieff did not say that Orage at the start taught us incorrectly. As far as his teaching went it was correct, but incomplete. It could be harmful if not related to other elements of the complete teaching, the next steps, so to speak. *That*, Gurdjieff promised to go into later: and in fact he did bring a fresh approach, but for the moment, he emphasized the way in which Orage had led us astray.

How could we understand what was really going on between Orage and Gurdjieff? What we saw we were unable to take in.

We were sure, by now, that knowledge as ordinarily thought of, though essential, could block the way to understanding by its didactic nature. What was the element lacking, since both Orage and Gurdjieff were apparently at odds?

If Gurdjieff held that Orage had given us not only useless but perhaps even harmful instruction, how did Orage answer that charge? Clearly Orage felt that he was not given what was promised him, and was acutely aware that he needed a new, deeper, more pervasive initiation both for himself and for those to whom he was a lifeline. This depended (Orage thought) on Gurdjieff's willingness to give him the material he needed, for the source, or the key to the source, was Gurdjieff. Orage was convinced that Gurdjieff was in possession of a knowledge of psyche and spirit that he yearned for and was ready for, and that Gurdjieff was deliberately refusing it.

This raised the old question of how much one has to rely on one's spiritual teacher for final knowledge, and the second important one: whether one was required to break into the source by oneself, because it could be earned only by intense inner effort. Ideas could be transmitted; even methods could be set down. From where, then, could the certainty that Orage sought be wrested?

It seems obvious enough that Orage thought, even believed, that it was within Gurdjieff's power to present it to him; with Gurdjieff's extraordinary gift of sorcery, he could produce in another whom he was readying for service the spiritual substance Orage hungered for. And the high level of ecstasy he had experienced in Fontainebleau was his evidence that the master intentionally brought about higher states in others, if he chose.

In Ouspensky's wonderfully honest account, he relates the moment when, after the greatest effort he was capable of, Gurdjieff released him, as though the limitations of Ouspensky's capacity had been reached. The same sort of questions seem to have arisen then in Ouspensky that arose later in Orage.

How difficult it is to judge one's teacher, especially in terms of one's own feeling of need. To be so close to the scent and feel refused the full fragrance is almost unbearable. On the one hand, Orage believed that he must follow his own star. Yet, on the other hand, he needed Gurdjieff's light to illuminate his path. In the end, he accepted his own way and trod it honorably. In the meantime, Orage's pupil-friends sensed his difficulty without truly understanding it and Orage insisted that we not take sides.

None the less the question remains with many of us still. One attempt to find an answer has to do with Gurdjieff's vision of a new and necessary harmony. Both Ouspensky and Orage were men of extraordinary intellect, who felt that final answers could be made by the unconditioned mind. They were both far from young when they met Gurdjieff. His teaching, and its continuation, depended on the harmonizing of all the centers, as he called them, head, heart and body. This harmonization was more profound than most Westerners could imagine, because it brought into action a relationship between the inner intelligences, which depend upon the capacity and operation of extraordinary attention. Gurdjieff had spent most of a lifetime learning this and making it his own. It could not be transmitted in verbal language, no matter how articulate, nor in mathematics, no matter how elaborate.

People of what we call good minds often think they can understand without themselves having the concomitant experience. What is true there? It may well be that a much subtler and more revolutionary change has first to take place in the whole of one's being before one is ready for the next step toward the state of consciousness we all seek.

On one occasion, Orage summed up the situation thus: Gurdjieff was his brother, who had gone off to strange countries and learned strange ways. None the less, they remained, in essence, brothers.

16
Conditions of work

I beg myself as well as my readers not to mistake understanding for attainment; and not to imagine, on the strength of their realisation of certain truths, that they possess them, or, still less, that they can use them. Our being, in which alone truth is possessed, is still a long, long way behind our understanding.   A. R. ORAGE

In the late fall of 1930, Orage wrote a number of us that he had taken passage on the SS *George Washington* for 29 December, which meant that he should arrive no later than the second week in January. Another letter, which he had written to Israel Solon, one of the 'gods' during Gurdjieff's previous stay in New York, was circulated among us, and is worth reading in full.

My dear Israel. I got your letter this morning and my first wish was to cable you my complete agreement with your attitude; but, on reflection, I find it better to write at some length and, in the meantime, to presume on your good judgement as you have already expressed it. I am very grateful for your expressions of personal friendliness which, as a fact, I could never doubt, if only for the reason that on my side, whatever is sincere and real in me is whole-hearted affection for you and the New York group. Whatever happens and whatever G. may do or require you and the group to do, I feel myself so personally knit with you that no thing can really sever our essential relations even if, externally, our paths should lie apart. What is more, I cannot conceive myself ever reproaching any one of you for anything you may find yourselves constrained to do or say. I know too well the difficulties of the situation to require any predefined line of conduct. You are like ships at sea in a storm, and the first principle of navigation is to get to port. So please, my dear Israel, do what you can to assure everybody that I beg them to think of and for themselves first and last. Their best 'loyalty' to me is to learn and to become all they can. I feel that 'loyalty' to me is confusing on still another ground. I came to New York as an agent of G. and the Institute idea – not at all in my own right or on my own responsibility. Certainly, however G. may say I have only titillated – I have done my best both for the group and for G. But if after these years G. himself comes along and, declaring that I have failed him as a good servant, proposes to take over the group himself, *or* to nominate a new agent in my place, I certainly have no complaint to make. I accepted this commission originally, I discharged it to the best of my ability, he is my superior officer and I quite naturally resign my commission at his suggestion, and all the more readily if he personally puts himself in my place. There is and can be thus, as you clearly see, no division of loyalty as between my superior officer and me. We must all, I as well as you, accept his rulings so long as we remain in his school.

But then another consideration arises. I've not been, in relation to the New York group, *just* an agent of G. Perhaps that has been my failure from his point of view. I should, perhaps have regarded the group as simply material for G.'s use in all respects, and had no such feelings about you all as would give me a qualm at whatever he might do. It *may* be, perhaps, that I should have treated you all like dogs (I don't mean harshly, of course), or, better to say, like a flock of sheep whose wool and mutton were of value to G. and one or two of whom might conceivably one day attain a higher state of being, *through* being used as wool and mutton by a presumed superman. Maybe it is so, and maybe any other attitude on my part (or that of any of G.'s agents) is titillation. My reply is simply that I couldn't either feel or pretend to feel in that relation. I, if you like to say so, fell in love with the group personally and so far from being willing to carry out my commission if it involved seeing the group shorn and encouraging it to grow wool, I found the shearing one prolonged agony; and in the end, I was more disposed to side with the group than with my master! Even now I am; and as you will see, it makes my situation really desperate. On the one hand, I believe that G. is our common teacher and the only one we are likely to encounter. But, on the other hand, I cannot make myself his agent when it appears to me to involve hurting you; and, furthermore, I cannot refrain from crying out to you at his approach – 'Look out! Be sure you get as well as give.' Certainly don't consider *me*, but be sure also that you do consider yourselves. For *he* is among you who perhaps doesn't care two hoots whether you fare well or ill, provided only that collectively you serve his aim (which incidentally is not personally selfish at all) *and* at the same time are offered individually a chance, if only a bare chance of possible 'salvation'.

The last consideration I will state is this. It is obvious that my unwillingness to go to all lengths for G., with the group and with myself, indicates an insufficiency of what shall I say? – faith in him? trust? radical conviction that he can do no wrong? Well, to be explicit, that is the fact. I have not that absolute faith. If I were Nahom and G. commanded me to slay my first born, I wouldn't do it. I realize that this degree of faith is perhaps essential to full participation in G.'s teachings. I realize that any degree of belief, short of this makes all services to him ultimately conditional and therefore, except within limits, not to be counted upon. I know it is not the 'Other-Self-Trust' which results from or leads to the sacred rite of eternal friendship. I regret that I have not got it in relation to G.; and I envy those who have or who may find it born in them. But while I wish it for others, I have sorrowfully to avow that I haven't got it myself; nor do I see myself attaining it by any means that I can employ. 'Lord', I can say, 'I believe'; but I have to add, 'Help thou my unbelief', because, in truth, my belief is not absolute.

I hope you will find these notes a sufficient reply to your letter, and, also, of some use to all the people who really feel the poignancy of our common situation. You are, of course, at full liberty to use this letter as you please. I have nothing to conceal from you all; and I am so far from feeling 'disloyal' to G. himself that, if it were feasible, I would sent him a copy of this letter myself. I can see clearly that from *his* point of view, believing in himself so absolutely, my half or three-quarters belief in him is titillation, and results only in the titillation of others. He *cannot* but wish either that I shall be absolutely faithful, *or* cease to be regarded or to regard myself as his chief 'minister' in America. I accept this without reproach. But what I pray for is that my own friends, the best I have on earth, the New York group, may not only not suffer on my account, but that, through me, like another Moses, they may find themselves led to the Jordan and transported across by Joshua Gurdjieff!

We must gain and not lose by the situation, Orage continued to advise us by letter. Gurdjieff had long ago promised us that he could bring us conditions of work, but that we had to understand for ourselves in order to make the right use of those conditions. 'Look how Gurdjieff has enriched us,' Orage said, 'His method I continue to regard as the Word of God,' Orage wrote to us later, 'His system I regard also as probably the very latest word of truth.' His use of the qualifying word 'probably' reflects the caution that was a characteristic ingredient of his opinions, and makes unequivocal the sentence that precedes it.

Shortly after we heard that Orage was on his way to New York and would soon be here, we were summoned to another meeting. The center of gravity of this meeting was a letter addressed to Orage, read aloud by Gurdjieff's new secretary, a German woman named Louise Goepfort. Here it is, as it appears in Gurdjieff's book entitled, *Life is Real Only Then, When 'I Am'*:[1]

I, the undersigned, after mature and profound reflection, without being influenced by anyone else at all, but of my own free will, promise under oath not to have, without instructions from MR GURDJIEFF or a person officially representing him, any relations whatsoever, spoken or written with any of the members of the former group existing till now under the name of 'Orage's group' of the followers of MR GURDJIEFF'S ideas and also not to have any relations without the special permission of MR GURDJIEFF or his substitute with Mr Orage himself.

I am to have relations exclusively with those members of the former group, a list of whose names will be given to me during the general meetings of the newly formed exoteric group.

We were to think it over and to sign the letter by noon the following day. To me, all this had much of the quality of theater. Several of my friends queried me at once about my intentions. When I replied that I would not sign the letter, they answered sadly that they would continue to care for me but would have to avoid seeing me from then on. There was much ado and taking sides, so much so that I left, not at all sure that I would be there the next day.

Muriel Draper, who had missed the session, telephoned me to find out what had taken place. When I asked what she would do, she responded, 'I would sign it at once, but of course I wouldn't pay the least attention to it.' Her attitude seemed to me sane and knowledgeable. What a relief it was after all the dramatic hubbub. I felt immediate respect for Muriel's common sense, and her unerring courtesy.

I recalled an evening when we were waiting for Gurdjieff to arrive in her living room full of faded, handsome furniture mixed with awkward contemporary bits and, at the back, a handsome throne. As he entered the room, Muriel rose and offered him the throne, which was the only comfortable chair. 'You sit there, Mrs Trapper,' Gurdjieff said, in the way he always pronounced her name. 'This is your house.' Muriel shook her equine head. 'No, Mr Gurdjieff, this is your house. I am honored to be a guest in your house.'

The moment of decision was to be noon the next day. But for some reason or other, it was put off, probably because too many people wanted to understand better what lay behind the demand. Some tried to reach Orage on the boat by telephone. It would be safe to say that most of the group members preferred to wait for Orage's arrival. At any rate, that is how the scenario went on. I had a strong presentiment about Orage's response.

As soon as he was ashore, he asked to see Gurdjieff and lost no time in meeting him. Orage was shown the letter, which he read with the closest attention. Then he signed it, the first to do so. I don't know whether others were astonished, but I was certainly not. It was no news to me that he wished not to be 'that Orage', but his more essential self, and if there was a possibility to reach that, he would endorse anything that would help him.

From then on, Orage was present at meetings. Though he was now presumably an 'ordinary member', he filled the same role as before. The word 'ordinary' had a special significance for us, and we could reflect on it. Many times it was emphasized that people who were considered by the world as extraordinary were often monstrous, that is to say, over-developed in one center at the expense of the others.

Ouspensky quotes Gurdjieff as having said that most people fall into three general classes: tramps, who have no values; lunatics, whose values are unreliable; and householders, whose sense of values is based on sane, instinctive knowledge of what we are. When the word 'normal' is used in the Gurdjieff teaching, it does not mean 'average'. It means, when applied to a human being, functioning as he should according to his nature.

Since most of us are, from this point of view, abnormal, the first necessary step is to become 'ordinary', that is, well-balanced and not monstrous. In a word, becoming ordinary is a necessary prelude to the state of harmonious being, which for Gurdjieff was the goal of human beings.

When the dust had settled from the episode of the letter, Gurdjieff divided us into three groups. Those who worked in one were not to know what was going on in the others; it may even have been that Orage was taking part in all three. The division was intended for those able to receive, respectively, esoteric, mesoteric or exoteric instruction, and people were placed in appropriate groups. Many have since said that they regarded this period of work under Gurdjieff as the most valuable they had yet received. He instructed a number of people in new ways of approaching the primary work of awareness, but after about a month of this, Gurdjieff returned to Fontainebleau.

Orage stayed on in New York that spring teaching a writing group he had begun the year before, and preparing a series of lectures on Social Credit. Sometime early in April 1931, he gave five talks on the subject to a mixed audience of his old group members and many people who were new to us. We tried, and tried hard, to grasp what the socialization of credit would mean. We began reading books he recommended, and many others, on economics, a field that had previously held little allure for most of us.

After Orage left us in the late spring of 1931, a number of those who had heard his lectures on Social Credit formed a 'New Economics' group, to begin to read the literature on economics and try to understand the monetary theory of Major C. H. Douglas, founder of the Social Credit movement. They had access to Orage's lecture notes, and began most seriously to study the various proposals economists were making to restore the general situation to something more bearable.

That is not to say, however, that it was Orage's interest alone that stimulated ours. The country was sinking to the nadir of the economic depression. Many of us, and the people we knew, including the extremely well-trained and educated, were out of work. There were breadlines in the city and desperate men were selling apples on street corners. All we could see was the murkiest of futures for ourselves and our compatriots.

One need not be a specialist to grasp what was clear to many ordinary people. It could be that even the power-possessors would take the trouble to listen to Major Douglas, an engineer whose professional work on international projects – dams, bridges – led him to an acute diagnosis and a practical cure for the world's economic illness. This was the moment to try to awaken people to their economic good. So though most of us were far from experts, we were quite sympathetic to Orage's concern for the economic welfare of the West.

17
Growing chungaree

Only what cannot be shaken is one's own.   A. R. ORAGE

After considerable reflection about their future, Orage and his family in the fall of 1931 had taken a house in London, on Hampstead Heath, a part of the city then practically a suburb. Whatever form his work was to take, he would add himself daily to the throng in the underground on their way to the city and, this, too, would be a new experience for Orage, now transformed into the good householder Gurdjieff commended to his pupils.

As soon as his old friends heard that he was settling in London, streams of welcomers and editorial offers began flowing towards Orage. Almost the first came from the *New Age*, which asked him to return as editor. There was a reservation, however: the publishers wanted assurances that he would never abandon it again, as he had done almost a decade earlier when he left it in search of God.

This time Orage's return to journalism was joined to an inner purpose he knew he would never swerve from, so he could not give his word to stay forever with the *New Age*. Now he was unequivocally faithful to the underlying unity which had guided him, through a network of paths, out of the dark wood he had encountered in the middle of the journey of his life. Orage's diversity was held together by that same unity in his continued adherence to the influence of the Gurdjieff teaching on his life. His chief concern was to find ways of serving the ideas and methods he was perennially grateful for. As he put it in a letter to Allan Brown, 'My ideal may be unrealisable, but I wish to

talk Gurdjieff without using a single spiritual or even philosophical phrase, – pure man-of-the-world vocabulary.'

Quite naturally, he could not promise to stay with the *New
Age*. His attitude toward service is not too dissimilar to the
tradition of the Bodhisattva who refuses to rest blissfully in
Nirvana as long as earth-beings remain huddled under the bur-
dens of unconsciousness. Now, in the midst of the widespread
economic disaster Orage had feared, as well as foreseen, he was
concerned to be an instrument in the service of economic health.
On 13 February 1932, he wrote to Allan Brown, to ask his help.

> I came back here to London, as you know, with a plan to
> recover the *New Age* and to use it as a means of propagan-
> dizing our ideas in relation to the world crisis. After a very
> complete survey of the situation, I've come to the conclusion
> that I had better start afresh and without the associations of
> the present *New Age*; and I am therefore proposing to found
> a new weekly journal, the *New English Weekly* – and to issue
> the first number in April. I have all the literary backing in
> the world for nothing; there is scarcely anybody I cannot get
> to write for me even without payment. But the financial
> backing is not so generous. I calculate that, for a year's trial,
> I need a guarantee of 1000 pounds or $4000; and of this sum
> I can raise, here, about half or three quarters. The rest I am
> trying to get from my American friends, and at least partly
> on the ground that I intend the paper to be as open to
> American writers and readers as to English.

A month later, in a letter of gratitude to his American friends,
he writes:

> I mean to try to make a Group organ of it, – very very
> carefully and elaborately disguised, but Group-work all the
> same. The *voice* will be intellectual, but the message will be
> from and to the heart, – if only I have the Grace of God.

From early in his life, Orage had been sensitive to the needless
suffering of the poor, to the cycle of unfulfilled lives that follow

so often from penury. Knowledge of the scale of such depriva-
tion reverberated in him as he saw that much of it originates less
from malice than from stupidity. In his youth, this vision made
him an idealistic socialist who, like Gurdjieff's Beelzebub,
wanted to reform the world in the direction he felt just. With
his gifts for public speaking, writing and editing, he endeavored
to convince his fellow countrymen, including those Gurdjieff
referred to as 'power-possessors', that they would all be better
off if they gave more intelligent thought to the problem of the
distribution of wealth.

However, the implementation of this idealism troubled him;
he looked for a practical way of bringing about the required
changes without producing class warfare and the other negative
results that follow revolutionary violence. When he began studying the economic ideas of Major Douglas, Orage felt sure he had
found a practical, non-violent way. It made sense to him that
the root of the purely economic problem lay in the mismanagement of credit; in the failure of those responsible for the creation
of money and credit to realize how much the power to change
or modify production and distribution lay with them.

Since, like the United States, Britain was going through a
major financial crisis, Orage thought to seize this moment to
bring about the realization that industrialism, with all the good
it produced, had led inevitably to unemployment.

Great respect though we in New York had for Orage's determination to influence a change in the financial structure, now
patently necessary to recovery from our present depression, we
were sadder and more uneasy about his absence. We were concerned about his present relation to Gurdjieff, upon which hung
for many of us, our continuation with the work. It may be that
Orage did not realize enough that he was a lifeline for many of
us, that it was he who had made possible our approach to
Gurdjieff and his teaching.

In this atmosphere, we could well understand Orage's wish
to return to his old trade as master journalist, and his preoccupation with starting a new journal. None the less, it was impossible for us to accept that we were parting with Orage, the
person we still turned to for help in understanding the Gurdjieff

teaching. As unanswerable questions arose, more of us took them to Orage by letter. In a reply to Israel Solon, and with inference to the rest of the group, Orage wrote on 23 January 1932:

> I'm disappointed that you and others found G.'s deprecation of self-observation discouraging, since his reason for his statement was familiar to you all. I never at any time said that there is, ready-made, an actual 'I' that can observe; but I always said – following Gurdjieff – that by feeding this conceptional I on self-observations (or, rather, by its own feeding) it develops as an embryo develops. The whole point of the method lay in its being a means to self-development; *not*, of course, to self-conception, this latter having been done for us, so to speak, and evidenced by the fact that our planetary body becomes fully formed. The *method* was to be practised by the conceived but not yet developed I; and it had to start from 'nothing', since only self-developed individuals rank as individuals. G. however had his own reasons for confusing your minds, no doubt. Only what cannot be shaken is one's own.
>
> I had a letter from him shortly after he arrived in N.Y. in which he advised me to be ready to undertake a task he would cable me about later. That is as far as he got; and I am still waiting. He may possibly write me on his return, but, on the whole, I think it very unlikely. I do not foresee for myself, in fact, any further personal association or even official association with G. I think I got to the end of my tether with him. This is no reflection, still being what I am, and conditioned in all senses as I am, I cannot go more than half a hog, let us say. I can regret it and wish that I had been different; but the fact remains that I cannot 'sell all' – and everybody – to follow G. in person. His method I continue to regard as the Word of God; I practise it to the best of my powers. His *system* I regard also as probably the very latest word of truth; but, as I cannot verify it myself, and have lost the hope that I ever shall be able; and as, furthermore, I cannot merely believe and, still less, try to persuade others of just my beliefs,

– I see no probability of my resumption of G. groups or teaching for the rest of my life. I hope some others of you may be able to go further. I'm not sorry I was the means of starting you; I'm only sorry I cannot continue with you and ahead of you. I have amongst the few *genuine* experiences of my life, such an affection for and such a tie with the New York group that I am eternally (that is, unalterably) grateful for that association. Say what G. may, it came more nearly to becoming a real Brotherhood (for me at least) than any other group of people I've met or actually heard of. And this association and tie remain lively in me, whatever may be your or my future relation with G. himself. As for coming to America, much as I should love to for these reasons, I do not see any place or work for me there, for the *other* reasons. I'm by no means 'at home' in London. So far, I have completely failed to get the sort of work I planned for myself. But I have several irons in the very slow fire, and one of them may be hot enough to use at any moment. At any rate, I expect to stay here more or less indefinitely and in the absence of the unforeseen. This is all, I think, that I need say for the moment in reply to your request for a statement.

The 'irons in the fire' were the means to start the new journal, which took some months to heat up. On 21 April 1932, the first issue of the *New English Weekly* appeared.

It shows something of Orage's genius for relationship with friends and colleagues that the *New Age* turned their annual dinner into a feast to welcome back Orage, now a competitor, and his new journal, which would be a friend to Social Credit. Most of his former associates greeted him with warmth, and more than a hundred of them attended the dinner. But he was quick to sense the undercurrent to the festive spirit of those who still resented what in their eyes was his former apostasy.

Mairet, who was there that evening, says that Orage finally won them over. 'His speech, which everyone so eagerly awaited, recovered at one blow his prestige in the Douglas movement and the confidence of older friends.' More interesting still is Mairet's impression of the changed Orage. 'Here was a new person, wielding all these powers to far more positive purpose: not charming us into his own circle of ideas. . . . Orage had returned from his wanderings a more integrated being than before.'[1] Thus was Odysseus welcomed back to a new Penelope, a journal now depending largely on American funds, at the depth of the depression in both countries.

In the first issue writers were unrestrained in their joy at having Orage back with them again to make demands upon their skill and their knowledge. Havelock Ellis declared that 'Never before were we more in need of guidance, at once thoughtful and vigorous, and directing the movement of civilisation. . . . For my own part, I give a warm welcome to the *New English Weekly*.' Artist Will Dyson, who felt Orage's absence as 'a loss to us both', wrote, 'Thank God you are returning to your natural business of elucidation and the breeding of elucidators.' Oliver St John Gogarty's response was, 'It is the same as hearing that, in one instance, at any rate, journalism is about to return to literature.' Sir Herbert Read said that 'Since you gave up the *New Age* there had been a gap in our literary life. I am convinced that when the literary history of the period between 1907 and 1922 comes to be written, your influence will be found to have run very deep and far.' Edwin Muir: 'The times are bad and the resurrection of the spirit of the former *New Age* at such an hour is doubly cheering, recalling to us that intelligence has a shaping power.'

Letters of joyous welcome arrived, ranging from novelists such as Michael Arlen and William McFee to the medievalist Eric Gill, and the poet Ruth Pitter, including Richard Aldington, the dramatic critic St John Ervine and many, many others.

The novelist Storm Jameson felt Orage's leaving as an uncomfortable gap which was not filled until, as she writes,[2]

a fine thing happened. This was in Berlin in the icy March of 1932, and I read in an English paper, standing in the street, cut by the bitter wind, that A. R. Orage was back. For a moment the dead came alive in me, only for a moment, for it is by these that we live.

In New York, the New Economics Group which had begun after Orage's series of lectures on Social Credit there, started a journal of its own devoted to politics and literature and espousing Major Douglas's Social Credit. The editors were Lawrence Morris and Gorham Munson, with Willem Nyland as publisher. They named the aspiring publication *New Democracy*. Though Orage had inspired it, the new journal was no mere imitation of the *New English Weekly*. It had its own American flavor and, before long, its own interested readers. When the province of Alberta in Canada undertook its own version of Social Credit, it was thought by some to have been influenced by *New Democracy*. (Later, Alberta's experiment met the not unusual fate of being considered a deviation by the orthodox Social Creditors.)

Naturally enough, there were many of Orage's old friends and group members who regretted Orage's departure, even criticized him as succumbing to a trait in his nature: that is to say, he was what Gurdjieff called a 'compassionate idiot'.

A Gurdjieffian ritual, which often preceded dinner when we were all together, was the toast to idiots. Though it was done with comic spirit, it was serious. Everybody was an *idiot* in the ancient Greek sense of each person having his own peculiarities, which differed from those of his neighbors. Thus there were round idiots, square idiots, hopeless idiots, who had the possibility of dying an honorable death, if they worked on themselves, swaggering idiots, zigzag idiots, who always went from one extreme to another, and one of the most congenial was the 'compassionate' idiot. But, as Gurdjieff explained his characteristics, he spoke of this idiot as helping a blind man across the street, but then looking up to see if his mother-in-law was watching him from her window. He did admit that there could be a sincerely compassionate idiot, but that was rare.

If Orage was, as many of us felt, the best sort of compassionate idiot, it was not astonishing that he was concerned with the economic state of things.

18
'When I am sick, I'm dead'

Orage's superiority over the men of his decade and over the prominent
or protuberant public figures and writers a decade or so older than
himself was that he pulled his weight. In an age of funking abuleia, or
passing the buck, he never waited for cats to jump, he never shirked
the responsibility of forming an opinion.   EZRA POUND

Some to consult him and others simply to be with him again –
a number of the old New York group members visited Orage
in London, and all returned with a powerful impression of his
general state. His wonderful intelligence, they reported, was
being applied to inform the world of what could be gained by
the socialization of credit.

We were increasingly sympathetic to this aim of his, since
what was happening in our own country raised bitter questions
about the management of money and credit by those in charge.
When in 1932, Franklin D. Roosevelt was elected president of
the United States, chiefly because he promised us a 'new deal',
he proceeded at once to close all the banks. After the agonized
inaction of President Hoover, who believed it was not the func-
tion of government to intervene in the private business of the
people, Roosevelt's incisive action, which one morning rocked
every town in the country like a seismic shock, released a wave
of hope. At any rate, the deathlike paralysis was broken, something was being 'done', though the underlying causes of the
depression remained untouched.

By the summer of 1933 a monetary conference was arranged
in London, which raised in some of us the hope that the primary
question of the creation of credit might at last be considered by
the experts.

My own reason for going to London that summer was less
inclusive: I simply wanted to see the Orage family to find out,
if I could, whether they would return again to America. Orage,

Jessie and young Dick were still living in Hampstead. Jessie was happily pregnant, this time hoping for a girl. Orage went daily to Cursitor Street in London to spend long hours working on the *New English Weekly*. To those of us who saw him that summer he reiterated his intention of giving more room to ideas on the level of the Gurdjieff teaching. He told us also that he had written Gurdjieff about his intentions.

Always he returned to the ever-present question of money and credit. It was necessary, he believed, to find a way out of the economic depression, and that there was a way. The socialization of credit would make it possible to solve the problem of distribution, which had taken the place of the age-old problem of production. That had been solved; modern industry and management could produce all that was needed. What was necessary now was the acknowledgment of the fact, and then the move in the direction of the right use of the means of distribution and, for that reason, he planned to devote his immediate efforts to popularizing the ideas of Social Credit. He had more than once compared the need to be concerned about radical economic measures with the need of a householder to go into the kitchen and put things in order, thus giving more essential concerns the room they deserved. For him, this was the time to go into the kitchen so that he might soon leave it and move into the arena of ideas on quite a different level.

Mairet agrees that Orage was looking forward to the moment when his particular gift for propaganda would no longer be required. Then, as Mairet says, 'His commentary on public affairs would be framed upon philosophic and psychological principles, with economics as only a secondary interest.'

But since at this moment he believed that the failure to create and distribute purchasing power at a rate in harmony with the expanding means of production was at the root of the world's economic misery, he felt he had to make the effort to interest others in a system of social credit, which would make change possible without violent revolution.

'. . . Money is, in one sense, a commodity like any other,' he wrote in an early issue of the *New English Weekly*:[1]

It happens, however, to be the one commodity whose employment as a 'carrier' is indispensable in every exchange of commodities that is not simple barter. The demand for it is therefore universal, and grows with the multiplication of goods and the occasions of their exchange. We are attributing no particular viciousness to the people who happen, by accident or ability, to find themselves in possession and control of this unique commodity, if we take it for granted that their attitude towards money is the attitude of most other monopolists to the object of their monopoly. That is to say, their attitude is one of self-preservation coupled with a lively anxiety for the maintenance of their paramount privilege.

In a vein that is so like the existing derogation of the financial experts that it could have been written this morning, Orage continues:[2]

It always happens that when Reason is despaired of, the fault is men's, and primarily, of course, of the representatives of the current Reason. . . . No doubt the expert in Finance answers to the demand for the application of the scientific method to the important province of life called Economics. But equally there is no doubt among sane people that these experts have sacrificed the whole of Reason to one faculty of Reason. As the majority of people have no skill in and cannot put their finger on what is deficient in the reasoning of the experts, they have no means of objection but to appeal for Men in place of them. Like the old lady who comforted herself with the thought that there was One Above Who would see that Providence didn't go too far, the people today call for Men to see that the Financial Experts do not go too far. It is the same thing as calling upon the Whole Reason to see that one of its parts, Scientific Reason, doesn't destroy us.

At lunch with Orage that summer in London, we found ourselves listening intently to the simplicity with which he spoke, the selection of telling phrases, the lucid way he led us artfully, yet wholly naturally, to inevitable new understanding, to some-

thing gained we had not before possessed. When asked about
his own life, he recounted the history of his long search for a
practical way, a just way of distributing wealth. After years of
weighing one form of socialism against the next, and always
with certain reservations about their practicality, he came in
contact with Major Douglas, and his idea of Social Credit. As
an engineer, he had seen in his own professional work the
stultification of credit hindering projects for the general welfare,
whether the scale was large or small.

'I had to wind a wet towel around my head,' Orage reminisced, 'to follow the mathematics of the banking system, of
Social Credit, and its ramifications. Finally I had no doubt that
the root of the problem lay in the mismanagement of money and
credit.' And then, having witnessed that his own prophecies of
the coming financial crisis had actually come about, he felt
urgently the need to make the economic truth more generally
understood.

From this special field, he led us as always to the human
dilemma, and we encountered again the limitations of our awareness, the blindnesses of our perception, all of it symptomatic of
the waking sleep in which we spent most of our lives. Do we
see anything in its proper relation to the whole? When we
examine our personal lives, how we are with those we care for,
are we ever able to be certain what they really need?

We left him that summer feeling Orage's tempered vitality. It
had been his intention from the start to open the *New English
Weekly* to the ideas closest to his heart; it seemed at last that he
would soon begin to give those his primary attention. He would
stay in touch with his American family, and keep his eye on the
development of the *New Democracy*, which was now gaining
readers.

In the summer of 1934 those who visited him assured us that
Orage was finding ways of continuing his connection with both
Gurdjieff and his teaching. One of Orage's oldest New York
companions and the editor of *New Democracy*, Lawrence Morris, spent some months in London and reported many of his
conversations with Orage on the subject that meant so much to
his old New York group. Again, in a letter written to John

Riordan on 1 October 1934, Orage refers to this dual purpose of his. He began the letter with a reference to a 'just pronouncement' he regarded as of the first importance, adding, 'I'll keep it by me against the time when I resume my Gurdjieff activities. At present,' he goes on to say,

> they are in suspense while I'm carrying out the 'task' of making the world credit-conscious! Larry [Lawrence Morris] will tell you all we've discussed; but I could have stayed longer. . . . Try to get Larry at least to report to you [the drastic conclusions] and believe me that they represent my best thought on the N.Y. group policy, past and future. (Parentheses mine.)

Early in the fall of 1934 he wrote to a number of people, including Mrs Jessmin Howarth, asking them to join him in a new venture. He had undertaken to supervise special work in Dartington Hall. Orage had always felt the importance of right education for the very young – and now with a boy and a girl of his own, his interest was personal as well.

When Mrs Howarth arrived in London, she and Orage talked together, leaving her with the impression that he intended, with Gurdjieff's permission, to have children in the school learn the Gurdjieff movements suitable for the young.

Orage had just been asked to broadcast a speech on Social Credit. This was to be the first time he would speak directly to the general public on the subject, and he wanted to weigh in advance each of the words of his short speech. So he suggested to Mrs Howarth that they wait until he had made the fullest use he could of this opportunity. Together they could then give the new school the thought it required.

Always a champion of the human voice as an instrument of communication, Orage looked forward to testing this with a radio audience. From the introduction of 'wireless', Orage had welcomed it as opportunity to give the human voice its due. Those of us in New York, as well as his English friends, were eager to know the effect of his talk, sponsored by the British

Broadcasting Company. The stage, that is to say the broadcasting studio, was set.

In all his years in New York, Orage had never seemed ill, never missed a meeting, never was tired. 'I am like a horse,' he once said, 'When I am sick, I'm dead.'

It turned out to be almost like that. For some time before the night of the broadcast, he had not been in his usual vital state and was abnormally fatigued. Breaking a precedent, he had suspended publication of the journal for a month and gone motoring in the country with his family. At the end he was ill, even had quite severe pain under the breastbone. But he went ahead with the broadcast, on the evening of 5 November.

The speech was, Mairet says, 'a masterpiece of popular and yet intimate exposition.' To read it today – when it is just as applicable to the world situation as it was forty-five years ago – is to recognize Orage's effort to bring home to all kinds of listeners a clear account of economic theory, as difficult for most of us to understand as the stock market or the gold standard.

'Imagine a plate-glass window stretching from John O' Groats to Land's End,' he said,[3]

> and, on the inside of it, all the goods that England makes, and, on the outside the forty or fifty millions of us still flattening our noses against the pane, just as we did when we were children.
>
> As it costs us nothing, let us enter the shop and have a look round.
>
> The first thing that strikes us is the staggering variety of the goods on sale. Nature is prolific in having created about half a million species of living creature; but the British genius has invented even more kinds of goods. . . . I happened to see that two hundred kinds of apple pie were put on the market this year; and one London store – you may be glad to hear – stocks no fewer than forty-three varieties of lipstick.

From the picture of the country as producer, he turned to the other side of the picture, moving from the shop of Plenty, to join the rest of the forty or fifty million would-be shoppers outside.

> What a change of scene! In contrast with the Productive system we have just left, where all is co-operation, reason and applied Science, we find a struggling mob in place of a disciplined army of technicians. Everybody seems to be fighting everybody else and most of us seem to be getting the worst of it.
> What is the trouble about?
> Let us not be self-deceived. You and I know very well. It's about Money.

From there he goes on, asking his listeners to stick to their own experience, to realize that Money is 'only a ticket authorizing you to go shopping in the emporium we just left.'
It takes an extraordinary synthesizing gift to make complex ideas simple, without reducing them to simple-mindedness: Orage struggled for that and succeeded.

> The stream of Price-values to the shop-window moves much faster than the stream of Money-tickets to the shopping public, with the result that the annual collective shopping tickets of the nation, called its Income, are insufficient to meet the collective annual Price-values created in its shop.
> Now this a matter of fact and not of theory; and it can be proved by simple arithmetic. Our shop-keeper . . . has told us that, at a rough estimate, our annual output of Price-values is ten thousand millions pounds and probably more. And our taxing officials tell us that our annual Monetary Income is about two thousand five hundred million pounds. As four is to one, so is our output of Price-values to the Money-tickets with which to meet them.
> Here, I believe, in this gap between Income and Prices, is the root-cause of our present difficulties.

It is interesting to compare the Social Credit solution with what is being said today by our experts in economics about the need for a 'negative income tax'. Toward the end of the talk, Orage throws the bomb, as it were, to the current banking system.

> Social Creditors believe that as the Wage-system becomes obsolescent, thanks to the progressive depopulation of Industry (what we call unemployment), Dividends should gradually take the place of wages; so that as the Machine displaces Men, the wage-income previously paid to the displaced men, continues to be paid to them by the Machine that has displaced them. If the Machine does the work of one hundred men, its production is obviously enough to pay one hundred men's wages. The Dividend is the logical successor to the Wage.

What is the 'negative income tax' other than a dividend? Orage ends realistically,

> I need not say that I do not expect you to accept these suggestions all at once. . . . But in conclusion, and by way of giving zest to your studies, I would only remind you of this historic date, and warn you that in the gap disclosed between Price-values and Income is enough gun-powder to blow up every democratic parliament.

Those who were with him at the studio noticed that, at one point during the talk, he paused longer than usual, and asked him afterwards what happened. He answered that he had not known before how clearly the mind can work with the body in severe pain.

Jessie and the little group of friends with them were anxious and, at the restaurant they went to after the broadcast, Orage promised that the next day he would see a doctor, a concession which, out of some quirk of pride, he had almost never made before. Instead of spending the night in the bedroom he and Jessie shared, he retired to his study where he often worked late. In the morning, when Jessie went into his study, she found him dead.

Stanley Nott notified the New York group at once, and Mrs

...r cabled back to Jessie, Orage's favorite quotation from ...ue *Bhagavad Gita*:

The wise grieve neither for the living nor the dead.
Never at any time was I not, nor thou,
Nor these princes of men, nor shall we ever cease to be.
The unreal has no being,
The real never ceases to be.

It was carved by Eric Gill on Orage's gravestone at the Old Hampstead Church, where the Dean of Canterbury, at his own request, conducted the tranquil church service.

Orage had said once with some emphasis that the *New English Weekly* would be his epitaph, and it was an exact prophecy. The issue after his death is an extraordinary tribute, not only to the writing and editing that were Orage's great accomplishment but to the man, who was that most unusual combination of brilliance and selflessness. The best writers and editors of England and America wrote eloquently of the editor, the critic and the man.

T. S. Eliot's summary is the most inclusive:[4]

Most of us have not the self-knowledge to realise how para-sitic we are upon the few men of fixed principle and selfless devotion, how the pattern of our world depends, not so much upon what they teach us, but just upon their being *there*. But when a man like Orage dies, we ought to admit that his no longer being *there* throws us, for the time, into disarray; so that a more thorough reorganisation is necessary than we would have believed possible.

Gurdjieff was with us in New York when the news came of Orage's death. After 1931, he had made several visits to the United States, and so was here in November 1934. Group members and old friends met with Gurdjieff and, in a room we had rented for meetings on Fifty-seventh Street, for a long time we sat together in silence. Then he spoke.

'How you say it in your country? May his soul reach the Kingdom of Heaven!'

I remember that evening well. There was a sight I was wholly unprepared for: Gurdjieff wiping the tears from his eyes with his fists, and saying to all of us:

'This man . . . my brother.'

Afterword

Five years after Orage's death, in 1939, war began again in Europe, and by December 1941 the United States had again joined the Allies. Peter and Sophia Ouspensky, who had settled in England in the early 1920s, left for the United States late in 1940, where they continued their approach to the Gurdjieff work with both English and American students.

Gurdjieff returned for the last time to America in December 1948, to repay what he sometimes called his debt to Americans – to people who under Orage's guidance had kept the Prieuré going until Gurdjieff closed it finally in the 1930s. During World War II, it had been these same Americans who sent money and food to him and to his pupils who risked gathering nightly in his flat during the blackouts of occupied Paris.

When the flow of support was finally stopped by the war, Gurdjieff charged necessities at neighboring merchants, assuring them that as soon as he had access to his 'oilwells' in America he would pay up. After the war, those cryptic oilwells gushed generously to redeem Gurdjieff's promise.

Less than a year after his visit, on 29 October 1949, Gurdjieff died, leaving his work in the hands of Jeanne de Salzmann. As he had wished, the Gurdjieff Foundation was set up in New York City. Veterans of Orage's groups and many of Ouspensky's pupils joined them. The work begun by Orage on Gurdjieff's behalf continues there today, under the guidance of Jeanne de Salzmann.

Notes

1 Arrival in America

1 CLAUDE BRAGDON, *More Lives Than One* (New York: Alfred A. Knopf, 1938), p. 321.
2 A. R. ORAGE, 'Henry James, and the Ghostly', the *Little Review*, August 1918. Also letter, spring number, May 1929.
3 C. DALY KING, *The Oragean Version* (privately printed, 1951).
4 PHILIP MAIRET, *A. R. Orage, A Memoir* (London: J. M. Dent, 1936), pp. 100–2.

2 Editor

1 PHILIP MAIRET, *A. R. Orage, A Memoir* (London: J. M. Dent, 1936), p. 16. (Republished with *Reintroduction* and *Afterthoughts*, by University Books, New Hyde Park, New York, 1966.)
2 So named after Fabius, Roman commander against Hannibal, whose policy was to wear out an enemy by employing cautious and dilatory strategy.
3 ROGER LIPSEY, *Coomaraswamy: His Life and Work* (Princeton University Press, 1977), p. 110.
4 STORM JAMESON, *No Time Like the Present* (London: Cassell, 1933), p. 90.
5 A. R. ORAGE, *Consciousness: Animal, Human and Superman* (London: Theosophical Publishing Society, 1907), p. 55.
6 A. R. ORAGE, *Nietzsche and the Dionysian Spirit of the Age* (London: Foulis, 1906); A. R. ORAGE, *Nietzsche in Outline and Aphorism* (London: Foulis, 1907).
7 PHILIP MAIRET, *A. R. Orage, A Memoir* (London: J. M. Dent, 1936), pp. 16, 17.

8   P. D. Ouspensky, *A New Model of the Universe* (New York: Alfred A. Knopf, 1931), pp. 305 *et seq.*

9   David Eder, *Memoirs of a Modern Pioneer* (London: 1949), p. 89.

10 There is a school today that calls itself 'psycho-synthesis'. Whether this bears any resemblance to Orage's idea is questionable.

11 P. D. Ouspensky, *A New Model of the Universe* (New York: Alfred A. Knopf, 1931), preface.

12 P. D. Ouspensky, *In Search of the Miraculous* (New York: Harcourt Brace, 1949).

13 P. D. Ouspensky, *Tertium Organum* (Manas Press, 1920, published many times since by Alfred A. Knopf, New York).

14 Claude Bragdon, *Four-Dimensional Vistas* (New York: Alfred A. Knopf, 1916).

15 Dhan Gopal Mukerji, Indian scholar and writer, wrote a popular book called *Caste and Outcast*, and a translation of the Indian classic, *Bhagavad Gita*.

3   Kitchen boy

1   Claude Bragdon, *More Lives Than One* (New York: Alfred A. Knopf, 1938), p. 321.

2   Denis Saurat, *La Nouvelle Revue Française*, vol. 41, chapter entitled 'Visite à Gurdjieff' (1 November 1933); Denis Saurat, *The Living Age* (Concord, N.H. & New York) chapter entitled 'A. R. Orage' (February 1935).

3   Stanley Nott, *Journal of a Pupil* (London: Routledge & Kegan Paul, 1961).

4   G. I. Gurdjieff, *All and Everything*; first series: 'An Objectively Impartial Criticism of the Life of Man', or, 'Beelzebub's Tales to His Grandson' (New York: Harcourt Brace, 1950). An earlier version under Orage's direct supervision was mimeographed and distributed to the Gurdjieff students in the early 1930s.

4   Inner fires

1   Margaret Anderson, *The Unknowable Gurdjieff* (New York: Samuel Weiser, 1962), p. 44.

2   Claude Bragdon, *More Lives Than One* (New York: Alfred A. Knopf, 1938), p. 324.

3   C. DALY KING, *The Oragean Version* (privately printed, 1951), p. 4.
4   ROBERT COURTNEY (pseudonym for C. Daly King), *Beyond Behaviorism* (New York: Grant Publications, 1927).

5   Cultivating the garden

1   THOMAS DE HARTMANN, *Our Life with Mr. Gurdjieff* (New York: Cooper Square Publishers, 1964), pp. 117 *et seq.*
2   Manuscript by Jean Toomer, written for and presented to Dr and Mrs W. J. Welch in 1956.

6   The buried bone

1   G. I. GURDJIEFF, *All and Everything*.
2   P. L. TRAVERS, *G. I. Gurdjieff* (Toronto: Traditional Studies Press, 1973).
3   STANLEY NOTT, *Journal of a Pupil* (London: Routledge & Kegan Paul, 1961).
4   THOMAS DE HARTMANN, *Our Life with Mr. Gurdjieff* (New York: Cooper Square Publishers, 1964).

8   Sound and image

1   *New English Weekly*, 21 July 1932, p. 329.
2   Ibid.
3   A. R. ORAGE, 'Economic Nationalism', *Fortune* magazine (New York: November 1933), pp. 56 *et seq.*
4   MURIEL DRAPER, *Music at Midnight* (New York: Harper & Bros., 1929).
5   HUGH FERRISS, *The Metropolis of Tomorrow* (New York: Ives Washburn, 1929). Also Jean Ferriss Leich, *Architectural Visions: The Drawings of Hugh Ferriss* (New York: Watson-Guptill Publications, 1980).
6   A. R. ORAGE, *Selected Essays and Critical Writings*, edited by Sir Herbert Read and Denis Saurat (London: Stanley Nott, 1935), pp. 125 *et seq.*
7   P. D. OUSPENSKY, *In Search of the Miraculous* (New York: Harcourt Brace, 1949), pp. 385, 386.
8   EDWIN MUIR, *An Autobiography* (New York: William Sloane, 1954).

9 A classical romantic

1 A. R. ORAGE, in *New Age*, 22 April 1926.
2 EDWIN MUIR, *An Autobiography* (New York: William Sloane Associates, 1954), p. 172.

10 Two rivers

1 A. R. ORAGE, *Psychological Exercises* (New York: Farrar & Rinehart, 1930).
2 MALCOLM COWLEY, *Exiles Return* (New York: Viking Press, 1951), p. 61.
3 A. R. ORAGE, *The Active Mind: Adventures in Awareness* (New York: Hermitage House, 1954).
4 The word 'flowers' was changed to 'blossoms' in the later editions of *Beelzebub's Tales to His Grandson*.

12 Limitation and expansion

1 Orage attributed this quotation to a Vedic saying.
2 A. R. ORAGE, *Psychological Exercises* (New York: Farrar & Rinehart, 1930).
3 ROM LANDAU, *God is My Adventure* (New York: Alfred A. Knopf, 1936), pp. 238, 239.

15 An end of patience

1 'Maize' has often been used as a religious symbol, sometimes as a growing stalk that reaches toward heaven. According to Edward S. Curtis in *Portraits From North American Indian Life*, 'A pinch of cornmeal tossed into the air as an offering to numerous deities of the Tewa, but especially to the sun, is a formality that begins the day and precedes innumerable acts of the most commonplace.' (New York: Promontory Press, 1972), p. XIV.
2 PHILIP MAIRET, *A. R. Orage: A Memoir* (New York: University Books, 1966), p. 107. (See chapter 2, note 1.)

16 Conditions of work

1 GURDJIEFF, *Life is Real Only Then, When 'I Am'*: the third series of *All and Everything* (New York: Triangle Editions, 1975), pp. 100, 101.

17 Growing chungaree

1 PHILIP MAIRET, *A. R. Orage: A Memoir* (New York: University Books, 1966), pp. 109–10. (See chapter 2, note 1.)
2 STORM JAMESON, *No Time Like the Present* (London: Cassell, 1933), p. 90.

18 'When I am sick, I'm dead'

1 *New English Weekly,* 28 April 1932, p. 31.
2 *New English Weekly,* 9 June 1932, p. 189.
3 A. R. ORAGE, *The BBC Speech on Social Credit,* broadcast 5 November 1934 (London: Stanley Nott, 1935), pp. 3, 5 *et seq.*
4 T. S. ELIOT, 'Orage: Memories', *New English Weekly,* 15 November 1934, p. 100.